I. Introduction

Young firms are often associated with an up or out dynamic. Young firms have high failure rates, but, conditional on surviving, young firms exhibit higher average growth rates as compared to older firms. These differential dynamics between young and old firms raise important questions. What is it about young firms which makes them unique? Do firm characteristics which differentiate between young and older firms also distinguish young firms that will grow rapidly from those that will not?

In this paper, we focus on one specific firm characteristic: the employee workforce. Labor and human capital are important components to production, especially in high-tech and innovative industries where startup activity abounds. This paper documents a number of new facts showing how employees differ at young firms, yielding insight into the characteristics and joint dynamics of young firms and young workers.

Using over a decade's worth of firm-level data from the U.S. Census Bureau, we find that young firms employ relatively more young workers. Around 27 percent of employees in firms aged 1 to 5 years are between 25 and 34 years old, and over 70 percent are under the age of 45. In contrast, in established firms that have been in existence for 20 years or more, fewer than 18 percent of employees are between the ages of 25 and 34, while almost half are over the age of 45. We find similar results when we control in a regression framework for firm size, industry, geography, and time. Furthermore, we document results consistent with causality. Following a plausibly exogenous increase in young workers, we observe an increase in new firm creation.

Young employees may be more likely to match with young firms for several reasons. Given younger employees will, on average, have had more recent education, they may possess more current technical skills. Building a workforce with such characteristics can be especially critical to young firms, especially those developing new products or establishing new methods of production. In addition, young employees may be a better fit for young firms due to the fact that younger employees are likely to be relatively more risk tolerant. Greater risk tolerance may make young employees more willing to bear the labor income and human capital risk of working for a young firm or to take on riskier projects within the firm.

In addition, young firms will employ more workers who have recently completed a job search by nature of being new. Young workers are likely to switch jobs early on in their careers as they acquire job and task specific skills and learn about their own skills and productivity (e.g., Johnson (1978), Topel and Ward (1992)). Thus, to the extent young workers make up a higher percentage of workers who recently completed job searches, they will be more likely to work at young firms, strictly as a function of the joint dynamics of young firms and young workers. Finally, young firms may disproportionately employ young workers due to assortative matching of workers and firms based on productivity or quality of workers and firms. To the extent that younger firms are, on average, less productive than older firms and younger workers are, on average, less productive than older workers, assortative matching would imply that less productive (young) workers would match to less productive (young) firms.

Each of these four mechanisms may explain part of the positive relation between firm age and employee age in the data. The intent of our analysis is not to identify one unique driver of the relation or even to provide a complete accounting of all the potential underlying mechanisms. Instead, we show how the evidence is consistent with three non-mutually exclusive mechanisms related to the unique skills, greater risk tolerance, and joint dynamics of young firms and young workers.

We document that the young firm, young employee relation is moderated but still significant when we limit the sample to new hires, a set of workers who have all recently undergone a recent job search. The reduction in the magnitude of the effect is consistent with the joint dynamics mechanism. Moreover, the fact that the relation still holds with new hires suggests multiple mechanisms are responsible for the employee age-firm age relation.

Considering wages of young firms and young employees, we find that young firms pay lower wages, on average, a fact consistent with the existing literature. However, interesting patterns emerge when we investigate by employee age. Young employees in young firms earn higher wages than young employees in older firms. Assuming wages proxy for human capital, this result is consistent with the unique skills mechanism and does not directly support the assortative matching mechanism.

Using firm outcomes, we document several more interesting correlations involving employee age. First, firms that are created with a larger share of young employees are more likely to subsequently raise VC financing. Given findings in Hellman and Puri (2000) that VC investors select more innovative firms, this result is consistent with young employees (those with recently acquired skills especially valuable for innovation) matching to more innovative startups. Second, young firms which employ relatively more young workers subsequently experience higher growth rates (conditional on survival) and, with some qualifications, higher failure rates. These results are consistent with the unique skills and greater risk tolerance of young workers mechanisms.

Finally, we ask whether the rate of new firm creation is affected by the supply of young workers. If young employees are important for young firm growth due to their unique skills or attributes, we should expect that when more young employees are available, entrepreneurs find it easier to start and grow young companies, especially in more innovative industries. Using historical demographic information on the relative ratio of youth in a state as a predictor for the ratio of younger to older workers ten or twenty years later, we argue that a causal relationship exists between the supply of young workers and the rate of new firm creation, especially in high tech industries, where innovation is greater. These results suggest that the supply of young workers, in addition to the supply of financial capital, is an important factor in the creation and growth of new firms.

Our study contributes to the literature on what drives new firm creation and growth. A large focus of this literature has been on understanding the role of financial market development and structure.[1] We explore the role of labor markets and how the relative supply of young workers can impact firm creation and growth. Our study is related to recent work by Lazear (2005), who examines the human capital traits of entrepreneurs and Doms, Lewis and Robb (2010), who show that there is more new firm creation in regions where the local labor force is more educated.[2]

Our results also contribute to the labor and organizational economics literatures in documenting the strong positive association between employee age and firm age and the narrower wage spread between older and younger workers at young firms. Previous studies have explored the relation between firm size and wages (e.g., Brown and Medoff (1989)) and between firm age and wages (e.g., Brown and Medoff (2003)), but none have examined the role of employee age in explaining the relation between firm size and age with wages. Moreover, our results are applicable to the organization economics literature which suggests that firm hierarchies might be flatter in young, entrepreneurial firms (e.g., Rajan and Zingales (2001)).

The remainder of the paper proceeds as follows. Section II reviews the relevant literature and considers four mechanisms that may underlie the positive relation between firm age and employee age and their associated empirical predictions. Section III describes the data. Section IV examines the relation between firm age and employee age. Section V considers evidence on the mechanisms underlying the relation. Section VI discusses sample selection issues. Section VII provides evidence of a causal relation between the supply of young workers and new firm creation. Section VIII concludes.

---

[1] See for example, Evans and Jovanovic (1989), Holtz-Eakin, Joulfaian and Rosen (1994) and Hurst and Lusardi (2004) for studies on the role of financial constraints, and Black and Strahan (2002), Hellmann, Lindsey and Puri (2008), and Puri and Zarutskie (2012) for studies on the role of specific financial institutions such as banks and venture capital.

[2] Our study is also related to the literature about how the characteristics and human capital of firm founders and top management teams relate to the characteristics and performance of the firms they join (e.g., Hamilton (2000) and Hurst and Lusardi (2004), Gompers, Lerner and Scharfstein (2005), Beckman, Burton and O'Reilly (2007), Graham, Harvey and Puri (2010), and Kaplan, Klebanov and Sorensen (2012).

II. Possible Mechanisms Underlying the Relation between Firm Age and Employee Age

In this section, we briefly review the related literature on firm age, employee age and firm and career dynamics. We then consider four mechanisms suggested by this body of work that may underlie the positive relation between firm age and employee age observed in the data.

A. Firm Age

Young firms exhibit different characteristics compared to older firms. Young firms are characterized by an up or out dynamic. For example, Dunne, Robertson and Samuelson (1989) show U.S. manufacturing plant failure rates decline with age as do the growth rates of non-failing plants. Using more recent data covering all industries in the U.S., Haltiwanger, Jarmin and Miranda (2012) also find that young firms have a high exit rate and, conditional on surviving, young firms exhibit higher growth rates as compared to older firms, controlling for size. These empirical patterns are consistent with models in which new firms enter with new business ideas or products and learn over time whether they can capture market share from incumbent firms (e.g., Jovanovic (1982) and Bhak and Gort (1993)).

Young firms are more likely to face constraints or high costs when accessing external capital, an empirical fact documented in many studies (e.g., Petersen and Rajan (1994), Hadlock and Pierce (2010)). Such constraints may make young firms more sensitive and vulnerable to oil price and credit market shocks, as shown in Davis and Haltiwanger (2001)[3], and economic downturns, as shown in Fort, Haltiwanger, Jarmin and Miranda (2012). The greater sensitivity of young firms to

---
[3] Age in Davis and Haltiwanger (2001) is measured at the plant level.

financial market conditions may also lead to some of the differences in characteristics and dynamics of young and old firms as shown in the theoretical setting of Cooley and Quadrini (2001).

Young firms are often credited with a disproportionate share of innovation, relative to their older peers. Using productivity growth as a proxy for innovation, Huergo and Jaumandreu (2004) find that innovation is highest at young firms and diminishes over time. Darby and Zucker (2003) describe industry dynamics where breakthrough innovation is concentrated in a few young firms. Christiansen (1997) documents through numerous case studies how younger firms are more likely to capitalize on disruptive innovations because of differences in their organizational structures compared to older firms.

B. Employee Age

Likewise, young workers display different behavior and characteristics compared to older workers. A large literature documenting the wage profiles of workers shows that wages tend to increase over the majority of a worker's lifetime (e.g., Ben-Porath (1967)) with a particularly sharp increase in the first 10 years of an employee's career (e.g. Topel and Ward (1992)). This upward sloping wage profile can reflect a variety of differences between younger and older workers and in how firms choose to compensate their employees. Younger workers may accumulate firm-specific experience and skills over time on the job (e.g., Becker (1962)). Johnson (1978) argues young workers have uncertainty as to their abilities and tastes – uncertainty that is not resolved until after sufficient job experience. As such, young workers are likely to try several jobs until they find a good match following which, presumably, wages will increase. Indeed, Topel and Ward (1992) find that in the first 10 years of a career, the average worker changes jobs seven times (accounting for approximately two thirds of total lifetime job changes) and Bjelland et al (2011) document higher employer to employer turnover among younger workers. Alternatively, this rapid increase in wages in the early stage of a worker's career has also been justified as evidence of a compensation plan where higher future wages discourage greater productivity and shirking today (e.g., Lazear (1981), Akerlof and Katz (1989)).

C. Mechanisms

In this section, we posit four non-mutually exclusive mechanisms which may explain, at least in part, the positive relation between firm age and employee age we observe in the data. For each mechanism, we also describe testable empirical predictions. Given the interconnected nature of these mechanisms, it is not surprising that several of these mechanisms yield similar predictions.

C.1. Skills

Since young employees are more likely to have recently completed their education, they may possess more current technical skills which allow them to have more innovative ideas or be able to better adapt to new environments.[4] Building a workforce with such characteristics may be especially critical to young firms, which may be developing new products or establishing new methods of production (e.g., Christiansen (1997)).

If unique skills are a key driver of the employee age-firm age relation, then we should find that young workers at young firm have higher human capital, on average, relative to young workers at older firms. In the absence of a direct measure of human capital, we proxy with employee wages and explore whether young employees in young firms receive greater compensation relative to young employees in older firms. Furthermore, if recently acquired skills are relatively more valuable for innovation, then we should find that the tendency of young firms to hire younger employees is stronger at more innovative firms. Finally, all else equal, the skills mechanism predicts young firms

---

[4] This point is argued in Lazear (1998). "Young workers bring new skills and new ideas with them into the firm. This is likely to be most important to industries that are undergoing rapid technological change. In these industries, new entrants have often learned the latest techniques through formal schooling. More senior workers who received their formal training many years prior may have well-honed job skills, but are unlikely to know as much about the most recent research as their younger counterparts." p.169-170.

with more young employees will be more successful, leading to lower firm failure and higher firm growth rates.

C.2. Risk Tolerance

Job loss can be extremely costly for workers and young firms are more likely to fail. Moreover, young firms are more sensitive to macroeconomic shocks, and firm failures during economic downturns are likely to be especially costly to workers as alternative employment options will be most difficult to find during these periods. Gibbons and Katz (1991) find that workers affected by plant closures experienced extended unemployment and lower average wages following the event. Sullivan and von Wachter (2009) document increased risk of mortality following plant closures and estimate a high-tenure male worker displaced at age 40 loses between 1 and 1.5 years of life.

As such, young firms may attract relatively more young workers due to the fact that young workers may be more risk tolerant. A number of studies in the psychology literature have found that younger people tend to be more risk tolerant (e.g., Vroom and Phal (1971) and Hensely (1977)). The economics literature has also argued that younger people may be less risk averse when it comes to portfolio choice (e.g., Bakshi and Chen (1994) and Bodie, Merton and Samuelson (1992)). Greater risk tolerance may make young employees more willing to bear the labor income and human capital risk of working for a young firm. Moreover, young workers may suffer less following displacement, consistent with von Wachter and Bender (2006).

Furthermore, greater risk tolerance may mean that young employees will be more likely to select riskier projects or tasks within the firm once they are hired, leading to both higher firm growth and higher probability of firm failures. If more risk tolerant younger employees select into riskier firms or chose riskier projects once employed, then we should observe more volatile outcomes at firms with more young employees.

C.3. Joint Dynamics of Young Firms and Young Workers

Young firms employ workers who have recently completed a job search by nature of being new. For example, a three year old firm can only employ workers who changed jobs in the last three years. Young workers are more likely to switch jobs early on in their careers as they acquire job and task specific skills and learn about their own skills and productivity relative to other workers and across jobs (e.g., Johnson (1978), Topel and Ward (1992)). Thus, to the extent young workers make up a higher percentage of workers who recently completed job searches, they will be more likely to be employed at young firms. Moreover, Jovanovic (1982) and Bhak and Gort (1993) argue that firms learn about their relative strengths and weaknesses over time. With this information, young firms then adapt, changing themselves to maximize future profits. This suggests that young firms may experience greater rates of employee turnover, as compared to more established firms, a prediction supported in Haltiwanger et al (2012). The presence of relatively greater churn at young firms will predict shorter employment tenures at these firms, strengthening the above prediction of more young workers at young firms.

Given this prediction depends critically on the assumption that young workers are relatively more likely to have engaged in a recent job search, a joint dynamics mechanism predicts a significant dampening of the young firm, young employee relation when looking at a sample of employees who have all recently completed a job search. However, after controlling for different frequencies in job searches, a learning by doing dynamic will still predict more young workers at young firms. Young workers joining the workforce learn about their own relative strengths and weaknesses over time, as in Johnson (1978). Older employees are more likely to know their skill sets. Given young firms are also learning and changing over time, older employees may be less inclined to work at these dynamic young firms. On the other hand, young employees who do not know their specific strengths and are looking to try different jobs may be more likely to join young firms, especially young firms that anticipate relatively greater learning and subsequent change. Jovanovic (1982) describes the outcomes from learning as either high growth or exit. As such, we expect young firms which attract more young workers to be associated with greater growth rates (for surviving firms) and greater exit rates.

C.4. Assortative Matching based on Firm and Worker Productivity or Quality

Oi and Idson (1999a, 1999b) argue that young firms are less productive, on average, as compared to more established firms. If young employees are also less productive, then assortative matching on firm and worker productivity would suggest that more young employees would match to young firms. If assortative matching is a key driver of the positive relation between firm age and employee age, then we should expect to see the young people who join young firms are of relatively lower average quality, as compared to the young employees who join older firms. If wages are a proxy for worker quality, then this should translate into relatively lower average wages for young employees in young firms compared to young employees in older firms. Likewise, we should expect to see the young firms with the greatest number of young of young employees are of relatively lower average quality, as proxied by lower growth and higher failure rates.

III. Data

We use four primary data sources in the analysis. We use data from the U.S. Census Bureau's Longitudinal Employer-Household Dynamics (LEHD) program to obtain information on the ages and wages of employees. We use data from the U.S. Census Bureau's Longitudinal Business Database (LBD) to obtain information on the industry, age and geography of the firms for which the employees in the LEHD work. We use Compustat to obtain additional information on the publicly traded firms in the sample. Finally, we use data from SDC Thomson's VentureXpert and DowJones VentureSource to obtain information on which firms in the LBD receive venture capital financing.

A. Longitudinal Employer-Household Dynamics Data

LEHD data is collected from the unemployment insurance records of states participating in the program. Data starts in 1992 for several states and coverage of states increases over time. By 2004, twenty-seven states in the U.S. are included in the LEHD data.[5] The LEHD data tracks employees who work for firms in the participating states on whom unemployment insurance taxes are paid.[6]

We use the Quarterly Workforce Indicators (QWI) which aggregates worker-level information in the LEHD to the business establishment level.[7] The QWI data provide information on the count and total payroll for employees hired and separated each quarter. This information is reported for all employees and by age groups. Age groups are reported in ten year intervals, e.g., age 25 to 34, age 35 to 44, etc. Total payroll includes regular salaries and all bonuses and commissions, as well as stock options and other equity compensation in some states.[8] Firms in the QWI are identified by their state employer identification numbers (SEINs). Information on the physical address, industry and federal tax employer identification number (EIN) of each business establishment is also recorded in the QWI. We annualize the QWI data by summing measures of flows, such as new hires and wages, over each quarter of a given year, and adjust wages to be in constant year 2005 dollars.

---

[5] These states are California, Colorado, Delaware, Florida, Iowa, Idaho, Illinois, Indiana, Kentucky, Maine, Maryland, Minnesota, Missouri, Montana, North Carolina, New Jersey, New Mexico, North Dakota, Oklahoma, Oregon, Pennsylvania, Texas, Virginia, Vermont, Washington, Wisconsin, and West Virginia.
[6] See Abowd et al (2006) for a more detailed description of the program and the underlying data sets that it generates.
[7] A business establishment is part of a firm defined by having a particular geographic location. For example, a law firm with an office in San Francisco and an office in Los Angeles would have two business establishments. Likewise, a manufacturing firm with three different plants operating in different locations, e.g., two in Illinois and one in Wisconsin, would have three business establishments.
[8] See http://www.bls.gov/cew/cewfaq.htm for additional details.

B. Longitudinal Business Database

The LBD is a panel data set that tracks all employer U.S. business establishments beginning in 1975.[9] The database is formed by linking years of the standard statistical establishment list (SSEL), a register of business establishments, maintained by the Internal Revenue Service of the U.S. Treasury Department. The LBD links the business establishments contained in the SSEL over time and assigns each a unique identifier as well as a firm-level identifier that allows researchers to aggregate information to the firm level. The LBD contains information on the physical location, industry, total employment and payroll for each business establishment.[10]

We use the LBD to track the business establishments of firms that are included in the QWI over our sample period 1992-2004. We measure firm age as time from first entry in the LBD, i.e., the year in which the firm hires its first employee. If a firm has multiple establishments, we take the age of the oldest establishment as the age of the firm, similar to the approach taken in Haltiwanger et al (2012). We can also observe the years in which an establishment exits the LBD. This allows us to identify firm shut downs. We classify a firm as exiting when all of its establishments leave the LBD, i.e., the firms' employment goes to zero.

We link business establishments in the QWI to the business establishments in the LBD using the Business Register Bridge. These files match business establishments across the two databases using federal EIN, industry, state, and county of the establishments. We then aggregate to the firm level using the firm-level identifier in the LBD. In Appendix Section A, we describe our matching methodology and the characteristics of the resulting sample in more detail.

---

[9] Data in the LBD comes from a snapshot of all establishments in the US taken once a year. As such, firms which exit within the first year of life may not be included in our sample. All of our results and conclusions apply only to those firms which we can observe. Haltiwanger et al (2012) argues such short-lived entrants account for a small fraction of total startups.

[10] For a more detailed description of the LBD see Jarmin and Miranda (2002).

C. Compustat, SDC Thomson and Dow Jones Data

We link information from Compustat to the Census data using the internal Census Compustat/SSEL crosswalk. This crosswalk assigns firms in the LBD to the firm-level data in Compustat using information on EIN and location of the business establishments. Compustat contains information from publicly traded firms' financial statements.

To link information from SDC Thomson (VentureXpert) and DowJones (VentureSource) on venture capital financings we employ the crosswalk developed by Puri and Zarutskie (2012), which employs a name and address matching algorithm to link to firms in the LBD. Specifically, we identify firms in the LBD as VC-financed if they can be matched to firms contained in VentureXpert or VentureSource and received VC financing over our sample period.

IV. The Relation between Firm Age and Employee Age

We first present the main fact in our paper - that younger firms employ more young workers – before turning to an examination of the mechanisms that may drive this relation. We examine the relation between firm age and employee age for our entire sample, which is dominated by smaller private firms, as well as for a subsample of public firms.

A. All Firms

Table I, Panel A reports the nonparametric relation between employee age and firm age in the full sample of 4,374,025 firms. The rows in Table I correspond to age categories for employees; the columns correspond to age categories for firms. The final column, Column (6), reports the average percentages for firms of all ages.

The QWI groups employees into age categories covering 10 years, beginning at age 14, and then groups employees aged 65 and older into one category. We consider the following employee age categories – between 25 and 34, between 35 and 44, between 45 and 54, and 55 or older. We collapse the upper distribution of ages to aged 55 or older for brevity, but find similar results when we consider the categories 55 to 64 and 65 to 99 separately. We do not consider employees younger than 25 throughout our analysis since many of these employees are still completing their educations and, thus, working part-time or in temporary positions. To the extent that firms (employees) have different preferences regarding part-time and temporary workers (employment), this sample will be biased.[11] Each cell reports the average percentage of employees in a given age category for firms in a given age category.

The striking fact that emerges from Table I, Panel A is that younger firms disproportionately employ younger workers. 26.9 percent of employees in firms aged 1 to 5 years old are 25 to 34 years old, as reported in Column (1). Furthermore, employees between 25 and 45 years old represent over half of the workforce at these young firms, totaling 54.9 percent of employees. The percentage of employees in the younger age categories falls steadily as we move across the columns and firm age increases. For firms older than 20 years in Column (5), employees aged 25 to 34 years account for only 17.5 percent of employment, and employees younger than 45 for only 42.2 percent of employment.[12]

B. Public Firms

Table I, Panel B reports the relation between firm age and employee age for the sample of 9,120 publicly held firms in the data. We examine public firms separately to see whether the employee age-firm age relation in the full population of firms is mainly driven by smaller firms with

---

[11] We report results only for workers over the age of 25. The youngest workers are likely to still be completing their educations and, thus, working part-time or in temporary positions. To the extent that firms and/or employees have different preferences regarding part-time and temporary workers and/or part-time and temporary employment, employees under 25 may exhibit different match rates by firm age as compared to workers over 25 years of age who are more likely to be working in full-time permanent positions.

[12] If we also include employees younger than 25 in the calculations, 70 percent of employees are younger than 45 in firms aged 1 to 5 years. For firms over 20 years, only 50 percent are younger than 45.

limited access to external financial markets. For the sample of publicly held firms only, we define firm age as time from initial public offering (IPO). To become publicly held, a firm must grow to a certain size as well as meet other regulatory criteria for its equity to be publicly traded. Therefore, the sample of publicly traded firms is tilted towards relatively more established and larger firms vis a vis the sample of all firms.[13]

For firms that have gone public 1 to 5 years ago, 35.4 percent of employees are aged 25 to 34. For public firms that have gone public over 20 years ago, only 23.8 percent of employees are aged 25 to 34. In contrast, for public firms that have gone public 1 to 5 years ago, 16.4 percent of employees are aged 45 to 54. For firms which have been public for over 20 years, this percentage rises to 23.8 percent. There is no strong pattern between employees aged 35-44 and firm age.[14] Thus, the employee-age firm-age relation is generally robust to the very different sample of larger public firms. In the next section, we test for statistical significance in a regression framework.

C. Controlling for Firm Size, Industry, Geography and Time

Table II tests whether the firm age-employee age patterns shown in Table I are robust to controls for firm size as well as year, industry and geography fixed effects. Table II reports estimates from OLS regressions of the fraction of firm employees in an age category on dummy variables for the 4 youngest firm age categories. The dummy variable capturing firms over 20 years is excluded from the regression. The coefficients on the firm age dummy variables should be interpreted as the difference between that age category and firms over 20 years. The regression also includes controls

---

[13] Summary statistics for the two samples are available in Appendix Tables A.III and A.IV.
[14] For the full sample, we find decreasing fractions of employees in the two youngest age groups by firm age and increasing fractions of employees in the two oldest age groups by firm age. For public firms, we continue to observe the same pattern with the youngest and two oldest employee age groups, however, we find a relatively flat relation between employees age 35-44 and firm age. The lack of robustness in the 35-44 age group may indicate the inflection point between younger and older workers resides in this age group.

for firm size, measured by the lagged natural logarithm of 1 plus total firm employees and industry (4-digit SIC code), state and year fixed effects for the full sample of private and public firms.[15,16] Panel A of Table II reports the results for all firms; Panel B reports the results for the sample of public firms.

Table II, Panel A shows that after controlling for firm size, industry, geography and time, the relation between employee age and firm age is strengthened. The fraction of employees age 25 to 34 is 9 percentage points higher in firms aged 1 to 5 compared to firms older than 20 years. This is an economically meaningful difference given that, on average, 23 percent of a firm's workforce is between 25 and 34 years of age, as reported in Table I. The percentage of employees aged 25 to 34 steadily declines as we move up the firm age categories. We also note that larger firms employ slightly more young workers.

Table II, Panel B shows that young public firms employ nearly 10 percent more employees aged 25 to 34, compared to the sample of firms over 20 years. There is a strong increase in the percentage of employees aged 45 to 54 and aged 55 or older as firms age. However, consistent with the raw data in Table I, there is no strong firm age pattern in the data for employees aged 35-44. The relation between the percentage of employees aged 35 to 44 is 2 percentage points lower at firms aged 1 to 5 vis a vis firms over 20 years.

Overall, we show that young firms disproportionately employ more younger and fewer older employees, a result that is robust to controls for firm size, industry, geography and year.

---

[15] We map NAICS codes to SIC codes for years 2002 to 2004.
[16] We also estimate logistic regressions in which the dependent variable is the log odds function of the fraction of employees in a given age category. We find our results are very similar to the OLS regressions in which the fractions of employees of a given age are the dependent variables and report these estimates for easier discussion of economic magnitudes.

V. Evidence on Mechanisms

In the previous section we documented a positive relation between employee age and firm age. In this section, we seek to understand the drivers of this relation by exploring related empirical evidence. We first look at the relation between firm age and age of new hires. Second, we explore average wages for young and older workers at both young and older firms. Next, we look at the relation between firms' potential for innovation and employee age. Finally, we explore the correlation between firm outcomes and employee age.

The intent of our analysis is not to identify one unique driver or even to provide a complete accounting of all the complex and jointly determined trends of young firms and young employees, a point emphasized by the fact that several of the identified mechanisms yield identical predictions. Instead, we document empirical evidence consistent with three non-mutually exclusive mechanisms. The results are consistent with the employee age firm age relation being driven, in part, by unique and valuable skills of young employees, greater risk tolerance of young employees, and the joint dynamics of young firms and young employees. Our analysis, however, does not allow us to definitively exclude alternative mechanisms that may also be at play, given the inter-relatedness of various explanations of the employee age, firm age relation and the complex nature of employee-firm job matching.

A.   *Evidence from New Hires*

The joint dynamics mechanism argues the young employee, young firm relation is driven, at least in part, by the fact that young firms can only employ workers who have recently completed a job change and young employees change jobs more frequently. Thus, after limiting the sample to new hires who have all done a recent job search, we should observe a weaker relation between firm age and employee age. We explore this prediction in Table III, Panel A using the full sample of all firms. In this table, the rows correspond to employee age categories (for new hires only) and the columns correspond to firm age categories.

First, we confirm the earlier assumption that younger workers make up a larger fraction of new hires. Column (6), which reports the age distribution of new hires averaged across all firm ages, shows that 50.5 percent of new hires are between 25 and 44 years of age, consistent with past findings. Second, we find a positive relation between age of new hires and firm age. Column (1) reports that 28.7 percent of new hires at firms aged 1 to 5 years are in the 25 to 34 year old category. Moving across the columns by firm age, we see a decline in the percentage of new hires aged 25 to 34. The percentage hits 25.3 when firms are aged over 20 years, as reported in Column (5). We see a similar pattern for new hires aged 35 to 44, but with a smaller decline in percentage hired as firms age. The percentage of new hires aged 45 to 54 is relatively flat across firm age and the percentage of new hires 55 or older more or less increases by firm age.

Table III, Panel B reports the relation between years since IPO and age of new hires for the sample of public firms. For firms that have gone public 1 to 5 years ago, 37.4 percent of new hires are aged 25 to 34. For public firms that have gone public over 20 years ago, only 30 percent of new hires are aged 25 to 34. In contrast, for public firms that have gone public 1 to 5 years ago, 13.3 percent of new hires are aged 45 to 54. For firms which have been public over 20 years ago, this percentage rises to 15.5 percent. Thus, the new hire employee-age firm-age relation is also present in the sample of larger public firms.

Table IV, Panel A shows that after controlling for firm size, industry, geography and time, the relation between new hire age and firm age is robust. Column (1) shows that the percentage of new hires aged 25 to 34 in firms aged 1 to 5 years is 3 percentage points higher than in firms over 20 years in the full sample of privately and publicly held firms. Table IV, Panel B shows the results are similar when looking just at public firms. Column (1) shows that the percentage of new hires aged 25 to 34 in firms that have gone public 1 to 5 years ago is 4.4 percentage points higher than in firms that have gone public over 20 years ago .

While we find a similar pattern between employee age and firm age when looking at new hires, the relation is less pronounced as compared to the sample of all employees. The more subtle relation in the sample of new hires is consistent with the joint dynamics mechanism. Moreover, the fact that we continue to observe a positive relation between firm age and new hire age is indicative that other mechanisms may also play a role in explaining the firm age-employee age relation.

Looking at just new hires provides insight into the mechanisms behind the young employee, young firm relation, however, we are only able to observe the age distribution of new hires at the sample of firms which are hiring. New hires will include new employees to fill new jobs (expansion hires) as well as new employees to fill jobs that were vacated by departing employees (replacement hires.) Since growing firms are hiring, by definition, this sample may be biased towards growing firms. On the other hand, Brown and Matsa (2013) find evidence indicating firms in distress experience higher employee turnover, suggesting declining firms may have large hiring needs as workers voluntary leave to seek out better opportunities.

If the sample of firms with new hires has an over-representative distribution of either growing or non-growing firms, this could bias our results if the relation between firm age and employee age depends on firm growth rates. However, this does not appear to be the case. As reported in Tables V and VI, we find similar correlations between firm age and new hire age in the sample of growing and non-growing firms – suggesting differences in growth rates for the set of hiring firms will not bias the results.[17]

B. *Evidence from Wages*

---

[17] There is a more complete discussion of the differences between the full sample and sample of firms with new hires in Section VI.

If young firms hire more young employees because young employees possess skills that are relatively more valuable to young firms, then young employees in young firms should receive greater compensation relative to young employees elsewhere. Moreover, young employees in young firms should earn compensation which is relatively more equal to their older colleagues, as compared to young employees at older firms. Alternatively, if positive assortative matching is driving the young employee, young firm relation then we should observe relatively lower wages for young workers at young firms.

We explore the relation between firm age, employee age and wages in Table VII. OLS estimates of the natural logarithm of the average wage per employee are reported for employees of all ages in Column (1) and for employees in a specific age category in Columns (2) to (5). The independent variables in the regressions include the 4 youngest firm age categorical variables as well as the lagged natural logarithm of 1 plus total firm employees, industry, state and year fixed effects. To preserve space, we only report the coefficient on the firms age 1-5 categorical variable which should be interpreted as the mean difference in the dependent variable for the youngest firm age category as compared to firms aged over 20 years, after controlling for firm size and industry, state and year fixed effects. Panels A and B explore wages for all firm employees. Panels C and D explore wages for new hires. Panels A and C use a sample of all public and private firms. Panels B and D use a sample of just publically traded firms.

We see in Table VII, Panel A, Column (1) that the average wage per employee, averaged across all employee age groups, is lower at firms aged 1-5. The average employee working for a firm aged 1 to 5 years old earns 6.2 percent less than the average employee working at a firm aged over 20 years. In unreported results, there is a steady increase in wages as firms age.

Moreover, when we decompose average wages by employee age, we see that the picture is more complicated. For younger employees, i.e., those under age 45, the average wage per employee is higher in young firms, as reported in Columns (2) and (3). On average, employees aged 25 to 34 earn 3.1 percent more and employees aged 35 to 44 earn 2.0 percent more at firms aged 1 to 5 years, relative to similarly aged employees in firms over 20 years old. We see a very different pattern for employees aged 45 and older in Columns (4) and (5). Employees aged 45 to 54 are paid almost 10 percent less and employees aged 55 or older are paid nearly 24 percent less in firms aged 1 to 5 years relative to firms older than 20 years. These large negative wage premia for older employees in younger firms contribute to the average effect observed across all employees in Column (1).

For public firms, as reported in Table VII, Panel B, the average employee at a firm which had its IPO in the last 1-5 years earns a higher wage, as compared to the average employee at a firm which had its IPO over 20 years ago. Furthermore, employees in the three youngest age groups all earn higher wages at the firms with the most recent IPOs as compared to similarly aged workers employed at the oldest firms. Employees aged 55 or older receive higher wages at firms which have been public for over 20 years vis a vis firms with recent IPOs.

These results are consistent with predictions of the skills mechanism. In contrast, these results do not directly support an argument that the firm age, employee age relation is attributed to a positive assortative matching mechanism.

While these wage results are consistent with the skills mechanism, they might also be explained by a tenure wage model. Lazear (1981) and Akerlof and Katz (1989) argue a firm may motivate young workers to work harder today at low wages if given the promise of higher future wages. Such implicit contracts will be more meaningful at firms where survival probabilities are higher.[18] Given older firms have higher survival probabilities, a tenure wage model will predict

---

[18] Becker (1962), Lazear (1981), and Akerlof and Katz (1989) document that at firms with a higher survival probability younger employees are paid relatively less with a promise of higher payment if they are promoted within the firm.

relatively lower wages for young employees and relatively higher wages for older employees at older firms.[19]

While we cannot completely exclude this alternative interpretation of the wage results, we document a number of results indicating a tenure wage model is not exclusively driving our results. For one, the tenure wage model predicts we should find a weaker pattern at public firms, given the difference in failure rates between young and old public firms is more modest relative to the comparable difference for private firms.[20] Instead, we find an even larger wage premium for younger employees at young public firms.

Second, a wage tenure model predicts the relation would be weaker when exploring wages of new hires only.[21] Looking first at new hires using the sample of all firms in Table VII, Panel C, we report that young new hires at young firms are paid relatively higher wages as compared to young new hires at firms over 20 years of age, consistent with the skills mechanism and a wage tenure argument. However, we also observe that older new hires receive higher wages at younger firms. This second finding is not consistent with either the skills or a wage tenure argument. This second finding is reduced when we exclude first year firms, which suggests that older workers who start new firms pay themselves well in the first year. Older workers who are subsequently hired at young but not first-year firms are not as highly compensated.

Moreover, for public firms where we expect to observe few if any of these nascent firms, we find more similar results between wages for all employees and just new hires, consistent with the skills mechanism. In Table V, Panel D, we report that younger new hires are paid relatively more

---

[19] Brown and Medoff (2003) find that the change in wages (from starting wage to date of survey) is higher per year of tenure at older firms, using a sample of approximately 1000 workers from the Survey of Consumers. They argue these results support a tenure wage model. These results are also consistent with our skills mechanism. Younger workers at younger firms will be hired at a higher starting wage given their relatively greater value to young firms.

[20] Bhattacharya, Borisov and Yu (2012) shows that mortality rates of public firms hit a peak at 6% for 3 year old firms, then decline to less than 2% for firms 20 years or older. Haltiwanger, Jarmin and Miranda (2012) shows that the exit rates of private firms hit a peak for firms 1-2 years old at 15% then declines to 2% for firms 16 years or older.

[21] New hires of older workers at established firms should not receive a wage premium (relative to new hires of older workers at young firms) given these employees have not built up tenure.

and new hires aged 55 or older are paid relatively less at firms which had an IPO within the last 5 years vis a vis firms which had an IPO more than 20 years ago. The age groups that command the highest wage premia in young public firms are new hires aged 25 to 34 years, who earn almost 10 percent more in young public firms, as compared to firms that went public over 20 years ago, and new hires aged 35 to 44 years, who earn 11.6 percent more.

C. Evidence from Firms' Potential for Innovation

If younger workers join young firms because their skills are especially important to innovation, then the skills mechanism predicts we should find young firms which are more innovative employ a relatively greater share of younger workers. Proxying for innovation in young firms is difficult as innovation often takes years to be observed. Thus, instead of measuring innovation directly, we use a proxy for future expected innovation – the attainment of VC financing. VC financing has been shown to be associated with rapid firm growth and innovation in the product market (e.g., Hellman and Puri (2000), Gompers and Lerner (2001), and Puri and Zarutskie (2012)).

In Table VI, we explore the relation between receiving VC financing and employee age at young firms. Columns (1) and (4) of Table VIII report marginal effects from probit models which estimate the probability a firm receives VC financing as a function of its initial characteristics. Fraction of employees aged 55 or older is the excluded group. The probit models are cross-sectional, and the number of observations is equal to the number of firms represented in each model. Column (1) estimates the probit model on all new firms in all industries. Given VC investment in concentrated in the "high tech" industries of Computers, Electronics, Biotech, and Telecom[22],

---

[22] See, for example Puri and Zarutskie (2012). These are the industrial categories typically used by databases such as VentureEconomics, which track VC investment activity. A firm is in the Biotech industry if its primary SIC code is 2830-2839, 3826, 3841-3851, 5047, 5048, 5122, 6324, 7352, 800-8099, or 8730-8739 excluding 8732. A firm is in the "Telecom" industry if its primary SIC code is 3660-3669 or 4810-4899. A firm is in the "Computer" industry if its primary SIC code is 3570-5379, 5044, 5045, 5734, or 7370-7379. A firm is in the "Electronics" industry if its primary SIC code is 3600-3629, 3643, 3644, 3670-3699, 3825, 5065, or 5063.

Column (4) estimates the probit model only on these industries. We find that having more employees aged 25 to 34 compared to the excluded group of workers aged 55 or older is associated with a higher chance of receiving VC financing in the future.[23] These results hold when considering all firms and just high tech industries. Having more workers in the age category of 35 to 44 as compared to workers over 55 is also positively associated with VC financing in both samples.

Assuming VC-financed firms need more cutting edge skills to innovate, as compared to non-innovative firms, then the results in Tables VIII consistent with the skills mechanism. However, we also acknowledge that firms which receive VC financing differ based on observable and unobservable characteristics and, thus, we cannot definitively exclude the possibility that these results are driven by an omitted variable correlated with VC financing and employee age. In the next section, we further test the relation between firm outcomes and employee age.

D. Evidence from Firm Outcomes

If young workers are more risk tolerant, as in Vroom and Phal (1971) and Hensely (1977), then we should expect that young employees match to the firms that present greater income or employment risk, such as those firms that display greater failure and growth rates. In Jovanovic (1982), firms learn that they are either efficient, in which case they grow, or that they are inefficient, in which case they exit. If young employees, who are also learning about their own skills, are relatively more likely to join firms that are learning about their abilities, then we should observe more young employees at firms with both higher growth rates and higher failure rates.

The skills mechanism suggests the same prediction regarding growth rates but the opposite prediction for failure rates. If young employees provide skills especially valuable to young firms, then we should observe higher growth and fewer failures among young firms with more young

---

[23] Because the probability of receiving VC is very low, less than 0.1 percent in the full sample of firms and only 1 to 5 percent in the sample of high tech industries, the magnitudes of the marginal effects are small in Columns (1) and (4).

workers. Furthermore, this should be especially true in industries where human capital is advancing most quickly, suggesting relatively greater value to more recently acquired skills. The assortative matching mechanism predicts more failures and lower growth at firms with more young employees.

In Columns (2) and (5) of Table VIII, we report estimates from probit models which predict whether a new firms fails within five years as a function of the age distribution of its initial labor force, its initial size, and industry, state and year fixed effects. Marginal effects are reported and the fraction of employees over 54 is the excluded group.[24] In Column (2), which estimates the model on all industries, we see that new firms with more workers aged 25-34, as compared to workers over 54, are more likely to fail. Alternatively, new firms with more workers 35-44, as compared to workers over 54, are less likely to fail. In Column (5), which estimates the model only on firms in high tech industries, we see that firms with more employees aged 25-34 and 35-44 are less likely to fail relative to firms with more workers age 55 or older. For all industries, Column (2), and high tech industries, Column (5), there is a strong relation between relatively more workers aged 45-54, as compared to workers aged 55 or older, and fewer failures. These results are consistent with the influence of multiple non-mutually exclusive mechanisms with competing predictions.

In Columns (3) and (6) of Table VIII, we regress the log of a firm's employment growth rate over the first 5 years as a function of the firm's initial labor force age distribution, total employment size, and state, industry and year fixed effects. The number of observations, or firms, drops in these regressions because firms must survive at least five years to be included in the analysis. We see that new firms that survive for 5 years and employ relatively more workers aged 25 to 34 and 35 to 44, as compared to workers aged 55 or older, grow more quickly. These results hold when looking at the

---

[24] The lower number of observations in Column (2) compared to Column (1) and in Column (5) compared to Column (4) of Table VI reflect the fact that we drop firms for which we cannot observe the five year failure rate due to right hand censoring of the data. We find similar results when we account for censoring using a hazard model estimation.

full sample of firms in Column (3) and when limiting the sample to high tech firms in Column (6). These results support the skills, risk and joint dynamics mechanisms.

VI. Sample Selection

Throughout the analysis, we make use of different subsamples. We limit the sample to just public firms (e.g. Table I, Panel B), firms which are hiring new workers (e.g. Table III), the cross-section of new firms (Columns (1) and (4) of Table VI), new firms which survive for 5 years (Columns (3) and (6) of Table VI), and firms just in high-tech industries (Columns (4) to (6) of Table VI). Repeating similar tests across various samples, such as comparing the firm age-employee age relation at all firms then at the sample of public firms, allows us to explore the robustness of the results. Focusing on sub-samples allows us to gain insight into the importance specific mechanisms. However, any interpretation is complicated given the sub-samples may differ along dimensions other than those highlighted in the tests. In this section, we discuss these concerns in more detail.

A. Public Firms

Most young firms are private. It is a unique feature of Census data and, subsequently of this analysis, that private firm are included. Since private firms dominate the full sample, we also repeat our analyses on the subset of public firms. Many research samples are limited to using public firms and this allows our results to be more directly comparable to these studies.

In the Appendix Table A.III, Panel A, we report summary statistics for the sample of all firms. In the Appendix Table A.IV, we report summary statistics for the sample of public firms. Public firms are larger, as measured by employee count, and pay higher wages, as compared to the full sample. The pattern is present in each firm age category. With public firms, we can also document additional firm characteristics. We report increasing firm size and leverage and declining Tobin's Q with firm age. Suffice to say, the sample of all firms, dominated by small private firms, and the sample of public firms are different on multiple dimensions. We argue that it is, therefore, quite striking that we find similar patterns between firm age and employee age across the two samples.

B. Firms Which Are Hiring

In the Appendix Table A.III, Panel B, we report summary statistics for the sample of firms which are hiring. As discussed in Section V.A., the sample of firms with new hires may differ from the full sample as these firms may be associated with different growth rates.[25]

Employee growth is defined as the annual change in firm-level employees divided by the average employment at the firm over the two years during which the change is measured, as in Haltiwanger et al (2012). To benchmark our employment growth results, we compare them to Haltiwanger et al (2012), however, a few differences between the samples complicate the comparison. For one, Haltiwanger et al (2012) drops first year firms from their analysis of growth and instead looks at growth rates for firms 2 years or older.[26] Furthermore, Haltiwanger et al (2012) use employee-weighted averages. We report establishment-weighted averages.

Similar to Haltiwanger et al (2012), we observe higher employment growth in firms under age 5. After age 5, there appears to be little to no relation between firm age and mean employment growth. We document a slightly lower mean employment growth rate, vis a vis Haltiwanger et al

---

[25] This is true only for the sample of private firms. 97% of the sample of public firms hires in a given firm-year, suggesting very little differences between the samples of public firms used in tests with all employees and tests with new hires.
[26] First year firms, where starting employment is 0, have a growth rate of 200% by definition.

(2012). The difference is likely due to the different averaging methodology. Haltiwanger et al (2012) note that, after controlling for firm age, firm size is positively correlated with employment growth.

We find a lower growth rate in Table A.III, Panel B when we limit the sample to hiring firms. This lower growth rate is likely due to a combination of some new hires constituting replacement hires and the nature of the composition of the data set. This difference in growth rates would be of concern to our interpretation if there are different patterns associated with replacement hires as compared to expansion hires. We explore this issue by repeating key tables in the paper and limiting the sample to either just growing firm or just non-growing firms. These results are reported in Tables V and VI. We find generally similar patterns in the sample of just growing and just non-growing firms. In particular, if we repeat the regressions in Table IV, Panel A using only growing firms, the coefficient on age 1-5 dummy is 0.034*** for new hires aged 25-34, 0.013*** for new hires aged 35-44, -0.007*** for new hires aged 45-54 and -0.023*** for new hires aged $\geq$55. If we repeat the regressions in Table IV, Panel A using only non-growing firms, the coefficient on age 1-5 dummy is 0.032*** for new hires aged 25-34, 0.001*** for new hires aged 35-44, -0.022*** for new hires aged 45-54 and -0.038*** for new hires aged $\geq$55.

C. Firms for which We Observe Wages

Additional sample restrictions apply when we consider wages. As long as a firm employs (hires) at least one worker, we can estimate the fraction of employees (new hires) in each age group. However, we need the firm to employ (have hired) at least one worker in a given age group to be able to estimate the average wages for employees (new hires) in that age group. As such, the relation between firm age and wages by employee age, involves different samples. Given the evidence in Table VI that firms which employ more young workers are different, the wage results we report in Table V could be biased.

We address this issue in Table VII, by exploring the relative wage premium between young and old workers employed at the same firm. We estimate the within firm difference in average wages per employee (new hires) between older workers (those aged 45 to 54 and 55 or older) and younger workers (those aged 25 to 34) and test whether this within firm wage differential can be explained by firm age. Table IX, Panel A presents estimates for the full sample of private and public firms; Table IX, Panel B presents estimates for the subsample of public firms. The regressions include industry, state and year fixed effects, and firm aged over 20 years is the omitted dummy variable.

In the full sample, we see that the wage differential between employees aged 45 to 54 and employees aged 25 to 34 is 15.7 percent lower for firms aged 1 to 5, as compared to firms aged over 20 years, as reported in Column (1). Moreover, there is an increase in the spread between these two groups of employees as firms age. The pattern is even more dramatic if we look at the wage differential between employees aged 55 or older and employees aged 25 to 34 in Column (2). When we focus on new hires in Column (3), we actually see that the wage gap between 45 to 54 year old new hires and 25 to 34 year old new hires widens in the youngest firms. However, this is driven by first year firms where older workers who begin their employment in the year of the firm's birth receive high wages. When we drop first year firms from the sample and only include firms aged 2 to 5 years, we see that the coefficient on the firm age 1-5 dummy becomes negative and significant at the 1 percent level. The wage spread between new hires 55 or older and new hires aged 25 to 34 also become significantly negative when we drop first year firms.

Focusing on the estimates for the subsample of public firms in Table IX, Panel B, we see that the spread in wages for employees aged 45 to 54 and employees aged 25 to 34 narrows by 5 percent for the firms which recently went public as compared to firms which went public over 20 years ago, both when we examine wages of all employees and of new hires only. The wage spread between workers aged 55 or older and workers aged 25 to 34 narrows by 20.9 percent and 11.6 percent for all employees and new hires, respectively, for the youngest vis a vis the oldest public firms.

These results indicate that the positive wage spread documented by labor economists between older and younger employees (e.g., Ben-Porath (1967) and Murphy and Welch (1990, 1992)) is narrower within young firms, with young employees earning relatively more equal pay with older employees in the same firm. This is consistent with the relative skill/productivity gap between young and older workers being smaller at young firms as compared to older firms. Moreover, the results are consistent with the earlier results, suggesting sample differences are not driving our results. However, we acknowledge that while these tests control for one bias (firms with different characteristics may hire different age workers), it introduces a different bias (to be in the sample, the firm must be hiring both old and young workers.)

D. Firm Fixed Effects

We primarily rely on cross-sectional variation for identification throughout our tests. While our data set consists of millions of firms, it contains at most thirteen years of data for a given firm. Perhaps young firms are not themselves unique but instead firms created in the 2000s (firms which will be included in the youngest age group) are different vis a vis firms created in the 1980s (firms which will be included in the oldest age groups) and these differences in firm characteristics over time are driving our results. To address this alternative interpretation of our results, we repeat key results after including firm fixed effects in the regressions. Including firm fixed effects in the regressions involves a trade-off. On one hand, by including firm fixed effects, we dramatically reduce the power of our tests due to the short time series available.[27] However, without firm fixed

---

[27] The average firm is observed for 4.6 years. This is partially driven by the high attrition rates of firms but it also greatly determined by the limited availability of LEHD data.

effects, we cannot exclude the possibility that our results are driven by changes in the distribution of firm characteristics over time.

In unreported results, we repeat Table II with firm fixed effects. With firm fixed effects, we still find a positive employee age-firm age pattern, albeit with weaker statistical significance. For example, we find that the share of workers aged 25 to 34 is 1.5 percentage points higher when firms are aged 1 to 5 years compared to when they are older than 20 years, when considering the full sample. This difference is 1.4 percentage points when estimated using the sample of public firms.

In unreported results, we repeat Table IV with firm fixed effects. We find that the share of new hires aged 25 to 34 is 0.3 percentage point higher when firms are aged 1 to 5 years, compared to firms older than 20 years, in the full sample of firms. For the sample of public firms, the difference is 0.6 percent, however, this difference is not statistically significant. Overall, we find weaker but still often significant results when looking at new hires using the full sample. We find insignificant differences when looking at new hires and the full sample. The loss of power is likely driven by the limited within-firm variation in age in this sample.

We also find that the wage results reported in Table VII Panel A are generally robust to the inclusion of firm fixed effects in the estimation. For example, in the sample of all firms, employees between 25 and 34 years of age receive wages 10 percent higher when employed at a firm aged 1 to 5 as compared to a firm over 20 years, on average. Wage results using new hires or public firms are weaker once firm fixed effects are included.

VII. Does the Supply of Young Workers Affect New Firm Creation?

In the previous sections, we showed that young firms disproportionately employ young workers and presented evidence that the unique skills of young employees, greater risk tolerance of young employees, and the joint dynamics of young firms and employees can partially explain this relation. If young employees are a critical component for young firms, then we should expect to find that exogenous changes to the supply of young workers affect new firm creation. In this section, we test this prediction.

We use the historic ratio of adolescents and young adults in the population as a proxy for the number of young workers in an area 10 or 20 years later. Specifically, we calculate the ratio of the population in a state between 15 and 24 years of age and between 5 and 15 years of age, as compared to the population between 15 and 54 years of age, using data provided by the US Census of Population. We find the historic ratio, lagged 10 years, is a strong predictor of age groups in the same state, after controlling for state fixed effects.[28] We argue this lagged ratio not only reflects the supply of young workers in a given state, but most importantly, is unlikely to be driven by current job opportunities, at least when used in a regression after controlling for time invariant differences across states.

The typical approach would be to use these variables as instruments in a two-stage least squares estimation. However, the Census does not provide state-level age distribution data from 1991 onwards. Thus, in order to maximize the sample years used in the estimation, we instead use the lagged age ratios directly as a proxy for the supply of young workers in a given state which is not likely to be driven by current job opportunities.

Table X presents the OLS regressions which predict new firm creation rates in a state and state-industry as a function of the fraction of the population aged 15 to 24, lagged by 10 years, or the function of the population aged 5 to 14, lagged by 20 years, as well as state and year fixed effects. The sample period in these regressions is 1980 to 2000. The first two specifications presents

---

[28] In an unreported regression, we find that the fraction of people aged 15 to 24 from 10 years prior is a significant predictor of people aged 25 to 34, with a coefficient of 0.8, using the available sample years of 1970 to 1990. We include state and year fixed effects in this regression.

estimates for new firm creation in all industries. We see that an increase in the fraction of the population that is young is associated with an increase in new firm creation rates. In particular, an increase in the fraction of the population aged 15 to 24 ten years ago by 5 percentage points is associated with an increase in the new firm creation rate of about half a percentage point. We find similar, but insignificant, results when we consider the fraction of the population aged 5 to 14 twenty years ago.

The remaining specifications estimate the impact of the share of youth in the population on new firm creation rates in the high tech industries of Biotech, Electronics and Telecom. We see that, in the case of Biotech and Electronics, an increase in the share of youth in population has a positive impact on new firm creation rates. For example, an increase in the share of youth in the population by 5 percentage points leads to an increase in the rate of new firm creation in the Electronics industries of between 1 and 2 percentage points. These results suggest that the supply of young workers does impact new firm creation, especially in industries in which unique skills of young workers are demanded by young firms.

The evidence presented in this section further supports the argument that young workers are a necessary ingredient for the creation and growth of new firms, due to their unique skills or willingness to work for new ventures, and buttresses our previous results that young, high growth, firms disproportionately hire younger employees and pay them higher relative wages.

VIII. Conclusion

We present large-scale evidence that young employees are an important component in the creation and growth of young firms. We first show that young firms disproportionately employ younger workers. Around 27 percent of employees in firms aged 1 to 5 years are between 25 and 34 years old, and over 70 percent are under the age of 45. In contrast, in established firms that have been in existence for over 20 years, fewer than 18 percent of employees are between the ages of 25 and 34, while nearly half are over the age of 45.

We argue that the positive relation between firm age and employee age is due, at least in part, to a combination of unique skills and greater risk tolerance of young employees, and the joint dynamics of young firms and young workers. Consistent with young employees having unique skills valued more highly in young firms, we find that young employees in young firms command higher wages than young employees in older firms and earn wages that are relatively more equal to older employees within the same firm. Further, we show that young employees disproportionately join young firms which have greater potential for innovation, as proxied by receiving VC financing. We present evidence that greater risk tolerance of young employees can partially explain the positive relation between firm age and employee age. We show that firms that hire young employees subsequently exhibit higher growth and, in some industries, higher failure rates. We also find evidence that the joint dynamics of young firms and young workers leads to greater matching of young workers to young firms.

Finally, we find evidence that the supply of young workers affects the rate of new firm creation, with fewer new firms being created when there are fewer available young workers in a region. Using historical demographic information on the relative ratio of youth in a state as a predictor for the ratio of younger to older workers ten and twenty years later, we argue that a causal relationship exists between the supply of young workers and the rate of new firm creation, especially in high tech industries.

Our findings also point to future research questions. How might the need to attract and compensate young employees, or employees who share similar attributes or skills, influence the organizational structure or compensation schemes used by young firms? How might it influence the financing choices of young firms or otherwise interact with financial constraints? Finally, what do shifting workforce demographics mean for new firm creation rates and their subsequent dynamics?

Appendix. Matching Establishments between the LEHD and the LBD and Sample Characteristics of the Matched Sample

In this Appendix, we describe how we match establishments in the LEHD to establishments in the LBD in more detail. We also discuss differences in the matched LBD-LEHD sample as compared to the full LBD and potential biases in earlier results associated with using different matching criteria or due to the time series properties of the LEHD data.

A. Matching Establishments in the LBD and the LEHD

We link business establishments in the QWI to business establishments in the LBD using the Business Register Bridge. The Business Register Bridge matches business establishments across the two databases using federal EIN, industry, state, and county of the establishments. The Business Register provides details to match observations based on 15 combinations of EIN, industry, state and county.[29] We use five of these matches based on EIN, industry, state and county as well as EIN, state and county. Over the period 1992 to 2001 we use SIC codes to match establishments by industry, and over the period 2002 to 2004 we use NAICS codes.

We first attempt to match establishments using the more precise industry information, e.g., EIN, state and county, and 4-digit SIC code or 5-digit NAICS code, and then relax the industry precision until we match establishments only on EIN and state and county. If multiple establishments in the LEHD match to one or more establishments in the LBD, we aggregate information for the LEHD establishments and assign this information to the aggregate LBD

---

[29] The combinations are EIN, 4-digit SIC or 5-digit NAICS, state and county; EIN 3-digit SIC or 3-digit NAICS, state and county; EIN 2-digit SIC or 2-digit NAICS, state and county; EIN 1-digit SIC or 1-digit NAICS, state and county; EIN, state and county; EIN 4-digit SIC or 6-digit NAICS and state; EIN 3-digit SIC or 4-digit NAICS and state; EIN 2-digit SIC or 2-digit NAICS and state; EIN 1-digit SIC or 1-digit NAICS and state; EIN and state; EIN and 4-digit SIC or 6-digit NAICS; EIN and 3-digit SIC or 4-digit NAICS; EIN and 2-digit SIC or 2-digit NAICS; EIN and 1-digit SIC or 1-digit NAICS; and EIN only. See Abowd et al (2006) for a more detailed description of the crosswalk files.

establishments to which they match. We then aggregate establishment-level variables up to the firm level to create a panel data set consisting of 4,374,025 firms tracked over the period 1992 to 2004, for a total of 20,185,572 firm-year observations.

Table A.I lists the percentage of matched establishments in the LEHD by matching criteria of EIN, state and county, and industry. The largest share of matches take place using the most detailed industry information. Over the period 1992 to 2001, 66% of establishments are matched using EIN, state and county, and 4-digit SIC code. Over the period 2002 to 2004, 58% of establishments are matched using EIN, state and county, and 5-digit NAICS code. Smaller percentages of establishments are matched based on less detailed industry information. The next largest share of matches are made using just EIN and state and county, with 13% of matches over the period 1992 to 2001 and 17% of the matches over the period 2002 to 2004 being made this way. We do not match based on coarser information than these combinations of EIN, state and county, and industry to ensure the relative accuracy of our matches.

Our matching procedure yields relatively high match rates. Table A.II. presents the percentage of establishments in the LBD that are located in states and years covered by the LEHD, and hence that could potentially be matched to the LEHD, that we do in fact match to LEHD establishments. Our overall match rate across all years is 63%, as seen in the last column of Table A.II. Match rates are higher over the period 1992 to 2001, ranging from 65% to 73%, compared to the period 2002 to 2004, in which match rates range from 49% to 55%. This likely reflect the addition of new establishments to the LBD in 2002 as well as less accuracy in industry and EIN matching amongst these new establishments. The match rates for establishments of public firms, i.e., those whose parent firms are matched to Compustat, have lower match rates, averaging 35%. This reflects the difficulty in matching establishments that are part of multi-unit firms, which may themselves have multiple EINs and operate in multiple locations and industry segments.

B. Comparing the Matched LEHD-LBD Data and the LBD

We next describe the characteristics of the matched LEHD-LBD data set and discuss possible sample selection biases. Table A.III, Panel A presents means of several key variables for the sample of firms that are used in the estimation of the employee age regressions in Table II, Panel A. Means are presented for all firms in the sample and also by firm age category.

We see that the average number of employees for a firm in the matched LEHD-LBD database is 26. The average firm has 22 employees in the broader LBD, as computed by the authors. This difference is statistically significance at the 1% level as determined by a difference in means t-test allowing for unequal sample variances. The average payroll per employee, reported in constant year 2005 dollars, for a firm in the LEHD-LBD panel of 27,249 is slightly lower than that in the full LBD of $31,000. This difference is statistically different at the 5% level as determined by a difference in means test allowing for unequal sample variances.

Although the differences in employment and wages between the matched LEHD-LBD sample and the broader LBD are statistically significant, they are of modest economic magnitude. The difference in firm size may be driven by the fact that the LEHD states tend to have larger firms vis a vis firms in non-LEHD states. These comparisons suggest that there are no major selection biases with regard to wages between our matched sample and the larger LBD.

Table A.IV presents means for the sub-sample of public firms in the matched LEHD-LBD sample. The average number of employees reported in the first row of Table A.IV reflects only the employees in the matched public establishments, and excludes those establishments in the same public firm that are not matched. The average, 2,938.5, is significantly smaller than the average number of employees at public firms over our sample period of around 10,000 employees.

When we examine firm characteristics taken from Compustat data, such as total assets and sales, however, we see that the public firms included in our sample are representative of the larger population of public firms over our sample period. Therefore, while we only observe employee characteristics in a fraction of the establishments in the public firms that we can match to the LEHD, the public firms included in the matched sample are representative of the broader population of public firms.

C. Does the LBD-LEHD Matching Criteria Used Matter?

As reported in Table A.I., more than half of our matched LBD-LEHD sample is created using the most stringent matching criteria. To confirm that including observations matched using less stringent matching criteria is not biasing our results, we repeat our employee age and wage regressions (Tables II, IV, and V) but only include firms that were matched using the most stringent matching criteria for all establishments, i.e., all establishments must be matched based on EIN, state and county, and 4-digit SIC code or 5-digit NAICS codes. We find our results are robust. For example, if we repeat the regressions in Table IV, Panel A using only observations which were matched using the most stringent match, the coefficient on age 1-5 dummy is 0.030*** for new hires aged 25-34, 0.007*** for new hires aged 35-44, -0.016*** for new hires aged 45-54 and -0.031*** for new hires aged ≥55.[30]

D. Do the Time Series Properties of the LEHD Matter?

A second possible concern with the LBD-LEHD matching is that states join the LEHD program at different times. As such, we have different time series properties for establishments located in different states. To ensure that the timing of states joining the LEHD does not bias our results, we repeat our employee age and wage regressions (Tables II, IV, and V) but restrict our sample to be a balanced panel of state-years from 1997 to 2004. We again find our results are robust.

---

[30] We chose not to clear these results to reduce the total number of samples submitted through the Census clearance process and due to the fact that the results were so similar to the estimates we report in the paper using all matched establishments.

For example, if we repeat the regressions in Table IV, Panel A using a sample with a balanced panel of state-years, the coefficient on age 1-5 dummy is 0.033*** for new hires aged 25-34, 0.011*** for new hires aged 35-44, -0.013*** for new hires aged 45-54 and -0.027*** for new hires aged ≥55.

References

Abowd, J., B. Stephens, L. Vilhuber, F. Andersson, K. McKinney, M. Roemer, and S. Woodcock, 2006, The LEHD Infrastructure Files and the Creation of the Quarterly Workforce Indicators, CES Technical Paper 2006-01.

Akerlof, G. and L.F. Katz, 1989, Workers' Trust Funds and the Logic of Wage Profiles. *Quarterly Journal of Economics*, 104(3):525-36.

Bahk, B., and M. Gort, 1993, Decomposing Learning by Doing in New Plants, *Journal of Political Economy*, 101:561-583.

Bakshi, G. and Z. Chen, 1994, Baby Boom, Population Aging and Capital Markets, *Journal of Business*, 67:165-202.

Becker, G.S., 1962, Investment in Human Capital: A Theoretical Analysis, *Journal of Political Economy, 70: 9 - 49.*

Beckman, C., Burton, D., and C. O'Reilly, 2007, Early Teams: The Impact of Team Demography on VC Financing and Going Public, *Journal of Business Venturing*, 22:147-173.

Ben-Porath, Y., 1967, The Production of Human Capital and the Life Cycle of Earnings, *Journal of Political Economy,* 75:352-365.

Bhattacharya, U., Borisov, A., and X. Yu, 2012, Firm Mortality and Natal Financial Care, working paper.

Bjelland, M., Fallick, B., Haltiwanger, J., and E. McEntarfer, 2011, Employer-to-Employer Flows in the United States: Estimates Using Linked Employer-Employee Data, *Journal of Business & Economics Statistics*, 29:493-505.

Black, S. and P. Strahan, 2002, Entrepreneurship and bank credit availability, *Journal of Finance,* 57:2807-2833.

Bodie, Z., R. Merton, and W. Samuelson, 1992, Labor Supply Flexibility and Portfolio Choice in a Life-Cycle Model, *Journal of Economic Dynamics and Control,* 16:427-449.

Brown, J., and D. Matsa, 2013, Boarding a Sinking Ship? An Investigation of Job Applications to Distressed Firms, working paper.

Brown, C. and J. Medoff, 1989, The Employer Size-Wage Effect, *Journal of Political Economy,* 97:1027-1059.

Brown, C. and J. Medoff, 2003, Firm Age and Wages, *Journal of Labor Economics,* 21:677-1697.

Christiansen, C., 1997, *The Innovator's Dilemma: When New Technologies Cause Great Firms to Fail*, Harvard Business School Press, Boston, MA.

Cooley, T. and V. Quadrini, 2001, Financial Markets and Firm Dynamics, *American Economic Review*, 91:1286-1310.

Darby, M. and L. Zucker, 2003, Growing by Leaps and Inches: Creative Destruction, Real Cost Reduction, and Inching Up, *Economic Inquiry*, 41:1-19.

Davis, S., and J. Haltiwanger, 2001, Sectoral Job Creation and Destruction Responses to Oil Price Changes, *Journal of Monetary Economics*, 48:465-512.

Doms, M., E. G. Lewis and A. Robb, 2010, Local Labor Force Education, New Business Characteristics, and Firm Performance, *Journal of Urban Economics,* 67: 61-77.

Duune, T., Roberts, M., and L. Samuelson, 1989, The Growth and Failure of U.S. Manufacturing Plants, *Quarterly Journal of Economics*, 104:671-698.

Evans, D. and B. Jovanovic, 1989, An Estimated Model of Entrepreneurial Choice under Liquidity Constraints, *Journal of Political Economy,* 97:808-827.

Fort, T., Haltiwanger, J., Jarmin, R., and J. Miranda, 2012, How Firms Respond to Business Cycles: The Role of Firm Age and Firm Size, working paper.

Gibbons, R. and L. Katz, 1991, Layoffs and Lemons, *Journal of Labor Economics*, 9:351-380.

Gompers, P. and J. Lerner, 2001, The Venture Capital Revolution, *Journal of Economic Perspectives,* 15:145-168.

Gompers, P., J. Lerner, and D. Scharfstein, 2005, Entrepreneurial Spawning: Public Corporations and the Genesis of New Ventures, 1986 to 1999, *Journal of Finance,* 60:557-614.

Graham, J., C. Harvey, and M. Puri, 2010, Managerial Attitudes and Corporate Actions, Duke University working paper.

Hadlock, C. and J. Pierce, 2010, New Evidence on Measuring Financial Constraints: Moving Beyond the K-Z Index, *Review of Financial Studies,* 23:1909-1940.

Haltiwanger, J., R. Jarmin and J. Miranda, 2012, Who Creates Jobs? Small vs. Large vs. Young?, working paper.

Hamilton, B., 2000, Does Entrepreneurship Pay? An Empirical Analysis of the Returns to Self-Employment, *Journal of Political Economy*, 108: 604-631.

Hellmann, T., L. Lindsey, M. Puri, 2008, Building Relationships Early: Banks in Venture Capital, *Review of Financial Studies*, 21:513-541.

Hellmann, T. and M. Puri, 2000, The Interaction between Product Market and Financing Strategy: The Role of Venture Capital, *Review of Financial Studies,* 13:959-984.

Hensley, W., 1977, Probability, Personality, Age, and Risk-Taking. *The Journal of Psychology*, 95:139-145.

Holtz-Eakin, D., D. Joulfaian, and H. Rosen, 1994, Sticking it Out: Entrepreneurial Survival and Liquidity Constraints, *Journal of Political Economy,* 102:53-75.

Huergo, E., and J. Jaumandreu, 2004, Firms' Age, Process Innovation and Productivity Growth, *International Journal of Industrial Organization* 22:541-559.

Hurst, E. and A. Lusardi, 2004, Liquidity Constraints, Household Wealth, and Entrepreneurship, *Journal of Political Economy,* 112:319-347.

Jarmin, R. and J. Miranda, 2002, The Longitudinal Business Database, CES Working Paper No. 02-17.

Johnson, W., 1978, A Theory of Job Shopping, *Quarterly Journal of Economics*, 92:261-277.

Jovanovic, B., 1982, Selection and the Evolution of Industry, *Econometrica*, 50:649-670.

Kaplan, S., M. Klebanov, and M. Sorensen, 2012, Which CEO Characteristics and Abilities Matter?, *Journal of Finance*, 67(3): 973-1007..

Lazear, E., 1981, Agency, Earnings Profiles, Productivity, and Hours Restrictions, *American Economic Review*, 71: 606-620.

Lazear, E., 1998, Personnel Economics for Managers, John Wiley & Sons, Inc, Hoboken, NJ.

Lazear, E., 2005, Entrepreneurship, *Journal of Labor Economics*, 23:4, 649-80.

Murphy, K. and F. Welch, 1990, Empirical Age-Earnings Profiles, *Journal of Labor Economics,* 8:202-29.

Murphy, K. and F. Welch, 1992, The Structure of Wages, *Quarterly Journal of Economics,* 107:285-326.

Oi, W. and T. Idson, 1999a, Firm Size and Wages, in *Handbook of Labor Economics, Vol IIIC*, edited by David Card and Orley Ashenfelter (Amsterdam: Elsevier), 2155-2214.

Oi, W. and T. Idson, 1999b, Workers Are More Productive in Large Firms, *American Economic Review*, 89:104-108.

Petersen, M. and R. Rajan, 1994, The Benefits of Lending Relationships: Evidence from Small Business Data, *Journal of Finance*, 49:3-37.

Puri, M. and R. Zarutskie, 2012, On the Lifecycle Dynamics of Venture-Capital and non-Venture-Capital Financed Firms, *Journal of Finance*, 67: 2247-2293.

Rajan, R. and L. Zingales, 2001, The Firm as a Dedicated Hierarchy: A Theory of the Origins and Growth of Firms, *Quarterly Journal of Economics,* 116:805-851.

Sullivan, D., and T. von Wachter, 2009, Job Displacement and Mortality: An Analysis using Administrative Data, *Quarterly Journal of Economics*, 124:1265-1306.

Topel, R. and M. Ward, 1992, Job Mobility and the Careers of Young Men, *Quarterly Journal of Economics,* 107:441-79.

Von Wachter, T. and S. Bender, 2006, In the Right Place at the Wrong Time: The Role of Firms and Luck in Young Workers' Careers, *American Economic Review*, 96:1679-1705.

Vroom, V. and B. Pahl, 1971, Relationship Between Age and Risk Taking Among Managers, *Journal of Applied Psychology*, 55:399-405.

Zingales, L., 2000, In Search of New Foundations, *Journal of Finance*, 55:1623-1653.

Table I. The Relation between Firm Age and Employee Age

Panel A reports the average percentage of employees in a given employee age group (row) by firm age category (column) for all firms in the union of the LEHD and LBD databases between years 1992 and 2004. Age is defined as time from first entry in the LBD. Panel B reports the average percentage of employees in a given employee age group (row) by firm age category (column), for public firms in the LEHD-LBD union that are matched to Compustat.

	\multicolumn{6}{c}{Firm Age}					
	Ages 1-5	Ages 6-10	Ages 11-15	Ages 16-20	Ages >20	All Ages
	(1)	(2)	(3)	(4)	(5)	(6)
Panel A - All Firms						
# of firms	2,557,082	1,609,913	1,066,899	912,421	741,075	4,374,025
# of firm-years	5,707,524	4,721,282	3,270,204	2,784,016	3,702,546	20,185,572
% of employees aged						
25-34 years	26.9%	24.2%	22.2%	21.0%	17.5%	23.0%
35-44 years	28.0%	28.1%	26.9%	25.3%	24.7%	26.9%
45-54 years	18.1%	20.3%	22.4%	23.0%	23.8%	21.0%
≥55 years	11.0%	13.5%	16.0%	19.6%	24.6%	16.1%

	\multicolumn{6}{c}{Years Since IPO}					
	1-5 Years	6-10 Years	11-15 Years	16-20 Years	>20 Years	All Years
	(1)	(2)	(3)	(4)	(5)	(6)
Panel B - Public Firms Only						
# of firms	1,969	2,949	3,032	3,371	3,422	9,120
# of firm-years	3,457	7,104	7,904	11,143	17,215	46,823
% of employees aged						
25-34 years	35.4%	33.8%	31.3%	28.8%	23.8%	28.7%
35-44 years	29.4%	30.1%	30.2%	29.9%	29.5%	29.8%
45-54 years	16.4%	17.3%	18.6%	20.0%	23.8%	20.5%
≥55 years	6.8%	7.6%	9.2%	10.9%	13.1%	10.6%

Table II. The Relation between Firm Age and Employee Age: Regression Analysis

Panel A reports OLS regressions using the fraction of employees in an age category as the dependent variable. The data are taken from the union of the LEHD and LBD data sets between years 1992 to 2004. Panel B reports OLS regressions using the fraction of employees in an age category as the dependent variable for public firms only. The data are taken from the set of firms that are matched to Compustat in the union of the LEHD and LBD databases between years 1992 to 2004. The independent variables in each regression, in both Panels A and B, are firm age categorical variables and the lagged natural logarithm of 1 plus total firm employees. The firm age category of over 20 years is omitted. Also included in each specification are 4-digit SIC code fixed effects, state fixed effects and year fixed effects. The unit of observation is a firm-year. T-statistics adjusted for clustering by firm are reported in parentheses. *** indicates statistical significance at the 1% level.

Panel A - All Firms

Dependent variable	(1) Fraction of employees aged 25-34	(2) Fraction of employees aged 35-44	(3) Fraction of employees aged 45-54	(4) Fraction of employees aged ≥55
Firm age 1-5 years	0.091 ***	0.040 ***	-0.053 ***	-0.145 ***
	(276.40)	(107.34)	(-145.58)	(-352.65)
Firm age 6-10 years	0.060 ***	0.037 ***	-0.029 ***	-0.114 ***
	(195.50)	(105.19)	(-82.86)	(-288.98)
Firm age 11-15 years	0.039 ***	0.023 ***	-0.008 ***	-0.086 ***
	(124.12)	(65.12)	(-21.99)	(-212.10)
Firm age 16-20 years	0.019 ***	0.008 ***	0.005 ***	-0.049 ***
	(66.83)	(25.52)	(14.28)	(-133.77)
Lagged log(1+firm employees)	0.020 ***	0.005 ***	-0.011 ***	-0.024 ***
	(212.23)	(46.01)	(-111.99)	(-222.06)
Industry fixed effects?	Yes	Yes	Yes	Yes
State fixed effects?	Yes	Yes	Yes	Yes
Year fixed effects?	Yes	Yes	Yes	Yes
N	16,343,058	16,343,058	16,343,058	16,343,058
R^2	0.050	0.015	0.029	0.088

Panel B - Public Firms Only

Dependent variable	(1) Fraction of employees aged 25-34	(2) Fraction of employees aged 35-44	(3) Fraction of employees aged 45-54	(4) Fraction of employees aged ≥55
Time from IPO 1-5 years	0.098 ***	-0.020 ***	-0.072 ***	-0.069 ***
	(19.37)	(-4.45)	(-18.33)	(-20.51)
Time from IPO 6-10 years	0.082 ***	-0.008 ***	-0.065 ***	-0.057 ***
	(25.14)	(-2.69)	(-23.82)	(-22.28)
Time from IPO 11-15 years	0.056 ***	-0.002	-0.047 ***	-0.042 ***
	(19.26)	(-0.70)	(-18.78)	(-18.35)
Time from IPO 16-20 years	0.028 ***	0.005 ***	-0.025 ***	-0.022 ***
	(13.29)	(2.47)	(-12.70)	(-12.95)
Lagged log(1+firm employees)	0.003 ***	-0.004 ***	-0.005 ***	-0.006 ***
	(4.90)	(-6.19)	(-7.41)	(-10.00)
Industry fixed effects?	Yes	Yes	Yes	Yes
State fixed effects?	Yes	Yes	Yes	Yes
Year fixed effects?	Yes	Yes	Yes	Yes
N	37,359	37,359	37,359	37,359
R^2	0.205	0.075	0.145	0.178

Table III. The Relation between Firm Age and Employee Age for New Hires Only

Panel A reports the average percentage of new hires in a given employee age group (row) by firm age category (column) for all firms in the union of the LEHD and LBD databases between years 1992 and 2004. Age is defined as time from first entry in the LBD. Panel B reports the average percentage of new hires in a given employee age group (row) by firm age category (column), as defined by years from IPO, for public firms in the LEHD-LBD union that are matched to Compustat.

	Firm Age					
	Ages 1-5	Ages 6-10	Ages 11-15	Ages 16-20	Ages >20	All Ages
	(1)	(2)	(3)	(4)	(5)	(6)
Panel A - All Firms						
# of firms	2,540,870	1,110,922	730,009	637,275	540,366	4,104,611
# of firm-years	5,106,216	2,900,703	1,987,184	1,685,182	2,309,702	13,988,987
% of new hires aged						
25-34 years	28.7%	28.1%	27.3%	27.3%	25.3%	27.6%
35-44 years	24.1%	22.2%	22.1%	21.9%	22.4%	22.9%
45-54 years	14.1%	12.9%	13.4%	13.6%	14.9%	13.8%
≥55 years	7.9%	7.5%	8.0%	8.6%	10.1%	8.3%

	Years Since IPO					
	1-5 Years	6-10 Years	11-15 Years	16-20 Years	>20 Years	All Years
	(1)	(2)	(3)	(4)	(5)	(6)
Panel B - Public Firms Only						
# of firms	1,976	2,862	2,932	3,277	3,388	9,007
# of firm-years	3,442	6,860	7,545	10,771	16,911	45,529
% of new hires aged						
25-34 years	37.4%	36.0%	34.9%	33.8%	30.0%	33.2%
35-44 years	26.0%	26.0%	25.4%	24.6%	24.9%	25.2%
45-54 years	13.3%	13.3%	13.6%	13.4%	15.5%	14.2%
≥55 years	4.5%	4.7%	5.0%	5.2%	6.4%	5.5%

Table IV. The Relation between Firm Age and Employee Age for New Hires Only: Regression Analysis

Panel A reports OLS regressions using the fraction of new hires in an age category as the dependent variable. The data are taken from the union of the LEHD and LBD data sets between years 1992 to 2004. Panel B reports OLS regressions using the fraction of new hires in an age category as the dependent variable for public firms only. The data are taken from the set of firms that are matched to Compustat in the union of the LEHD and LBD databases between years 1992 to 2004. The independent variables in each regression, in both Panels A and B, are firm age categorical variables and the lagged natural logarithm of 1 plus total firm employees. The firm age category of over 20 years is omitted. Also included in each specification are 4-digit SIC code fixed effects, state fixed effects and year fixed effects. The unit of observation is a firm-year. T-statistics adjusted for clustering by firm are reported in parentheses. *** indicates statistical significance at the 1% level.

Panel A - All Firms

Dependent variable	(1) Fraction of new hires aged 25-34	(2) Fraction of new hires aged 35-44	(3) Fraction of new hires aged 45-54	(4) Fraction of new hires aged ≥55
Firm age 1-5 years	0.032 ***	0.009 ***	-0.014 ***	-0.032 ***
	(90.17)	(27.00)	(-48.97)	(-121.39)
Firm age 6-10 years	0.020 ***	-0.004 ***	-0.018 ***	-0.027 ***
	(55.85)	(-11.83)	(-65.50)	(-107.20)
Firm age 11-15 years	0.011 ***	-0.005 ***	-0.012 ***	-0.020 ***
	(31.17)	(-13.33)	(-41.58)	(-76.32)
Firm age 16-20 years	0.005 ***	-0.004 ***	-0.006 ***	-0.011 ***
	(12.25)	(-10.30)	(-19.15)	(-41.79)
Lagged log(1+firm employees)	0.011 ***	-0.005 ***	-0.008 ***	-0.011 ***
	(121.07)	(-56.34)	(-111.05)	(-174.62)
Industry fixed effects?	Yes	Yes	Yes	Yes
State fixed effects?	Yes	Yes	Yes	Yes
Year fixed effects?	Yes	Yes	Yes	Yes
N	11,404,068	11,404,068	11,404,068	11,404,068
R^2	0.020	0.013	0.018	0.028

Panel B - Public Firms Only

Dependent variable	(1) Fraction of new hires aged 25-34	(2) Fraction of new hires aged 35-44	(3) Fraction of new hires aged 45-54	(4) Fraction of new hires aged ≥55
Time from IPO 1-5 years	0.044 ***	-0.015 ***	-0.036 ***	-0.018 ***
	(8.32)	(-3.23)	(-10.09)	(-8.79)
Time from IPO 6-10 years	0.030 ***	-0.008 ***	-0.026 ***	-0.017 ***
	(8.81)	(-2.63)	(-9.91)	(-10.30)
Time from IPO 11-15 years	0.024 ***	-0.008 ***	-0.018 ***	-0.014 ***
	(7.37)	(-2.74)	(-7.40)	(-9.29)
Time from IPO 16-20 years	0.014 ***	-0.001	-0.010 ***	-0.007 ***
	(5.58)	(-0.60)	(-5.30)	(-5.41)
Lagged log(1+firm employees)	-0.002 ***	-0.007 ***	-0.006 ***	-0.003 ***
	(-2.95)	(-11.21)	(-11.13)	(-8.72)
Industry fixed effects?	Yes	Yes	Yes	Yes
State fixed effects?	Yes	Yes	Yes	Yes
Year fixed effects?	Yes	Yes	Yes	Yes
N	36,384	36,384	36,384	36,384
R^2	0.090	0.041	0.057	0.059

Table V. The Relation between Firm Age and New Hire Age for Growing and Non-Growing Firms

The data are taken from the union of the LEHD and LBD data sets between years 1992 to 2004. This table presents robustness tests of the results reported in Table IV, Panel A. Panel A presents OLS regression estimates on a sample of growing firms. Growing firms include startups, or first-year firms, and older firms which have employment growth rates between 0.10 and 1, where employment growth is defined as the change in employment over two consecutive years divided by the average employment at the firm over the same time period. Panel B presents OLS regression estimates on a sample of non-growing and shrinking firms. Non-growing and shrinking firms are defined as those whose employment growth rates are zero or negative. The unit of observation is a firm-year. T-statistics adjusted for clustering by firm are reported in parentheses. *** indicates statistical significance at the 1% level.

Panel A - Growing Firms

Dependent variable	(1) Fraction of new hires aged 25-34	(2) Fraction of new hires aged 35-44	(3) Fraction of new hires aged 45-54	(4) Fraction of new hires aged ≥55
Firm age 1-5 years	0.034 ***	0.013 ***	-0.007 ***	-0.023 ***
	(58.21)	(23.30)	(-15.01)	(-56.45)
Firm age 6-10 years	0.021 ***	-0.006 ***	-0.018 ***	-0.024 ***
	(36.46)	(-11.92)	(-40.45)	(-61.48)
Firm age 11-15 years	0.012 ***	-0.006 ***	-0.013 ***	-0.018 ***
	(19.95)	(-9.88)	(-26.72)	(-43.20)
Firm age 16-20 years	0.004 ***	-0.004 ***	-0.006 ***	-0.010 ***
	(6.94)	(-5.92)	(-11.48)	(-23.23)
Lagged log(1+firm employees)	0.012 ***	-0.008 ***	-0.010 ***	-0.010 ***
	(86.40)	(-63.50)	(-93.02)	(-117.19)
Industry fixed effects?	Yes	Yes	Yes	Yes
State fixed effects?	Yes	Yes	Yes	Yes
Year fixed effects?	Yes	Yes	Yes	Yes
N	4,434,468	4,434,468	4,434,468	4,434,468
R^2	0.022	0.016	0.021	0.028

Panel B - Non-Growing and Shrinking Firms

Dependent variable	(1) Fraction of new hires aged 25-34	(2) Fraction of new hires aged 35-44	(3) Fraction of new hires aged 45-54	(4) Fraction of new hires aged ≥55
Firm age 1-5 years	0.032 ***	0.001 ***	-0.022 ***	-0.038 ***
	(61.43)	(1.89)	(-53.58)	(-105.19)
Firm age 6-10 years	0.022 ***	-0.001 ***	-0.018 ***	-0.031 ***
	(47.90)	(-2.19)	(-48.23)	(-91.93)
Firm age 11-15 years	0.014 ***	-0.003 ***	-0.012 ***	-0.023 ***
	(28.31)	(-5.66)	(-30.20)	(-66.47)
Firm age 16-20 years	0.006 ***	-0.003 ***	-0.006 ***	-0.013 ***
	(12.49)	(-6.33)	(-14.16)	(-36.62)
Lagged log(1+firm employees)	0.014 ***	-0.002 ***	-0.008 ***	-0.014 ***
	(94.86)	(-14.29)	(-62.90)	(-131.54)
Industry fixed effects?	Yes	Yes	Yes	Yes
State fixed effects?	Yes	Yes	Yes	Yes
Year fixed effects?	Yes	Yes	Yes	Yes
N	5,434,892	5,434,892	5,434,892	5,434,892
R^2	0.019	0.011	0.016	0.030

Table VI. The Relation between Firm Age and New Hire Age for Growing and Non-Growing Public Firms

The data are taken from the set of firms that are matched to Compustat in the union of the LEHD and LBD databases between years 1992 to 2004. This table presents robustness tests of the results reported in Table IV, Panel B. Panel A presents OLS regression estimates on a sample of growing firms. Growing firms include startups, or first-year firms, and older firms which have employment growth rates between 0.10 and 1, where employment growth is defined as the change in employment over two consecutive years divided by the average employment at the firm over the same time period. Panel B presents OLS regression estimates on a sample of non-growing and shrinking firms. Non-growing and shrinking firms are defined as those whose employment growth rates are zero or negative. The unit of observation is a firm-year. T-statistics adjusted for clustering by firm are reported in parentheses. *** indicates statistical significance at the 1% level.

Panel A - Growing Public Firms

Dependent variable	(1) Fraction of new hires aged 25-34	(2) Fraction of new hires aged 35-44	(3) Fraction of new hires aged 45-54	(4) Fraction of new hires aged ≥55
Time from IPO 1-5 years	0.042 ***	-0.021 ***	-0.034 ***	-0.016 ***
	(6.23)	(-3.66)	(-7.51)	(-6.08)
Time from IPO 6-10 years	0.025 ***	-0.010 ***	-0.031 ***	-0.017 ***
	(5.46)	(-2.42)	(-9.71)	(-8.91)
Time from IPO 11-15 years	0.018 ***	-0.013 ***	-0.020 ***	-0.014 ***
	(4.21)	(-3.42)	(-6.56)	(-7.98)
Time from IPO 16-20 years	0.011 ***	-0.001 ***	-0.010 ***	-0.009 ***
	(3.19)	(-0.31)	(-3.90)	(-5.76)
Lagged log(1+firm employees)	-0.005 ***	-0.008 ***	-0.006 ***	-0.003 ***
	(-4.91)	(-8.55)	(-8.62)	(-5.74)
Industry fixed effects?	Yes	Yes	Yes	Yes
State fixed effects?	Yes	Yes	Yes	Yes
Year fixed effects?	Yes	Yes	Yes	Yes
N	13,686	13,686	13,686	13,686
R^2	0.129	0.067	0.082	0.094

Panel B - Non-Growing and Shrinking Public Firms

Dependent variable	(1) Fraction of new hires aged 25-34	(2) Fraction of new hires aged 35-44	(3) Fraction of new hires aged 45-54	(4) Fraction of new hires aged ≥55
Time from IPO 1-5 years	0.032 ***	0.004 ***	-0.036 ***	-0.023 ***
	(2.97)	(0.38)	(-4.76)	(-5.67)
Time from IPO 6-10 years	0.031 ***	-0.012 ***	-0.021 ***	-0.016 ***
	(5.45)	(-2.18)	(-4.44)	(-5.46)
Time from IPO 11-15 years	0.025 ***	-0.003 ***	-0.018 ***	-0.013 ***
	(5.08)	(-0.73)	(-4.45)	(-5.17)
Time from IPO 16-20 years	0.016 ***	-0.003 ***	-0.012 ***	-0.006 ***
	(3.82)	(-0.70)	(-3.48)	(-2.72)
Lagged log(1+firm employees)	0.000 ***	-0.007 ***	-0.007 ***	-0.003 ***
	(-0.43)	(-6.82)	(-7.18)	(-5.50)
Industry fixed effects?	Yes	Yes	Yes	Yes
State fixed effects?	Yes	Yes	Yes	Yes
Year fixed effects?	Yes	Yes	Yes	Yes
N	14,682	14,682	14,682	14,682
R^2	0.058	0.030	0.040	0.043

Table VII. Wages by Employee Age and Firm Age

Each column shows results from an OLS regressions estimated using the log wage (in year 2005 dollars) per worker in a given category as the dependent variable. Column 1 includes all employees. Columns 2-5 restrict the sample to employees in a given age group. The independent variables are firm age categorical variables (i.e., firm age 1-5 years, firm age 6-10 years, firm age 11-15 years and firm age 16-20 years) and lagged natural logarithm of 1 plus total firm employees. The firm age category of over 20 years is omitted. Included in each specification are 4-digit SIC code fixed effects, state fixed effects and year fixed effects. Only the coefficient on firm age 1-5 years and Time from IPO 1-5 years are reported to conserve space. The unit of observation is a firm-year. The data are taken from the union of the LEHD and LBD data sets between years 1992 to 2004. Panel A reports results for all employees using the full sample of privately and publicly held firms. Panel B reports results for all employees in the sample of publicly held firms only. Panel C reports results for the wages of new hires only using the full sample of private and public firms. Panel D reports results for the wages of new hires only using the sample of public firms only. T-statistics adjusted for clustering by firm are reported in parentheses. ***, **, and * indicate statistical significance at the 1%, 5% and 10% levels, respectively.

Panel A - All Firms: Wages of All Employees

	(1) Log(wage/employee) all employees	(2) Log(wage/employee) aged 25-34	(3) Log(wage/employee) aged 35-44	(4) Log(wage/employee) aged 45-54	(5) Log(wage/employee) aged ≥55
Firm age 1-5 years	-0.062 ***	0.031 ***	0.020 ***	-0.094 ***	-0.239 ***
	(-53.72)	(22.96)	(13.97)	(-59.21)	(-123.54)
N	16,336,715	9,565,061	10,615,733	9,509,330	7,881,437
R^2	0.280	0.213	0.227	0.234	0.230

Panel B - Public Firms: Wages of All Employees

	(1) Log(wage/employee) all employees	(2) Log(wage/employee) aged 25-34	(3) Log(wage/employee) aged 35-44	(4) Log(wage/employee) aged 45-54	(5) Log(wage/employee) aged ≥55
Time from IPO 1-5 years	0.064 ***	0.175 ***	0.216 ***	0.126 ***	-0.067 **
	(2.34)	(7.33)	(8.20)	(4.47)	(-2.02)
N	37,359	36,402	36,781	36,526	35,141
R^2	0.206	0.208	0.217	0.211	0.176

Panel C - All Firms: Wages of New Hires

	(1) Log(wage/new hire) all employees	(2) Log(wage/new hire) aged 25-34	(3) Log(wage/new hire) aged 35-44	(4) Log(wage/new hire) aged 45-54	(5) Log(wage/new hire) aged ≥55
Firm age 1-5 years	0.127 ***	0.079 ***	0.123 ***	0.121 ***	0.131 ***
	(107.78)	(55.49)	(78.71)	(65.76)	(56.93)
N	11,355,225	6,269,452	5,664,829	4,104,194	2,760,070
R^2	0.209	0.199	0.203	0.193	0.171

Panel D - Public Firms: Wages of New Hires

	(1) Log(wage/new hire) all employees	(2) Log(wage/new hire) aged 25-34	(3) Log(wage/new hire) aged 35-44	(4) Log(wage/new hire) aged 45-54	(5) Log(wage/new hire) aged ≥55
Time from IPO 1-5 years	0.044 *	0.099 ***	0.116 ***	0.029	-0.067 **
	(1.83)	(4.94)	(4.81)	(1.11)	(-1.98)
N	36,384	34,863	34,679	33,161	28,655
R^2	0.147	0.147	0.142	0.122	0.098

Table VIII. Initial Employee Age and New Firm Outcomes

Columns 1 and 4 report probit estimates which predict whether a firm ever receives VC financing. Columns 2 and 5 report probit estimates which predict whether a firms fails within 5 years of being started. Marginal probabilities are reported followed by z-statistics in parentheses for these probit models. Columns 3 and 6 report OLS regressions estimates in which the log 5 year employment growth rate, for surviving firms, is the dependent variable. The dependent variables in all models are the fraction of employees in a given age category over 55 years is the omitted group. Also included in each model are the fraction of employees younger than 25 years, the lagged natural logarithm of 1 plus total firm employees as well as 4-digit SIC code fixed effects, state fixed effects and year fixed effects (estimated for each firm in its first year of existence). The data in column 1 is taken from the union of the LEHD and LBD data sets between years 1992 to 2004 and is limited to firms that enter the LBD between 1992 and 2004. The sample in column 2 is further limited to exclude firms for which we cannot observe 5 years of data due to right hand censoring. The sample in column 3 is further limited to include only firms which survive for 5 years. Columns 4 to 6 mirror the regressions in columns 1-3 after limiting the sample to just firms in high tech industries. High tech is defined to include Biotech, Telecom, and Computer and Electronics. A firm is in the "Biotech" industry if its primary SIC code is 2830-2839, 3826, 3841-3851, 5047, 5048, 5122, 6324, 7352, 800-8099, or 8730-8739 excluding 8732. A firm is in the "Telecom" industry if its primary SIC code is 3660-3669 or 4810-4899. A firm is in the "Computer" industry if its primary SIC code is 3570-5379, 5044, 5045, 5734, or 7370-7379. A firm is in the "Electronics" industry if its primary SIC code is 3600-3629, 3643, 3644, 3670-3699, 3825, 5065, or 5063. ***, **, and * indicate statistical significance at the 1%, 5% and 10% levels, respectively.

	All Industries			High Tech Industries		
	(1) Receives VC	(2) Fails within 5 Years	(3) 5-year Employment Growth rate	(4) Receives VC	(5) Fails within 5 Years	(6) 5-year Employment Growth rate
Fraction employees aged 25-34 in firm's first year	0.00074 *** (10.76)	0.014 *** (5.50)	0.285 *** (42.52)	0.0018 *** (4.99)	-0.024 *** (-2.83)	0.326 *** (12.56)
Fraction employees aged 35-44 in firm's first year	0.00068 *** (9.15)	-0.026 *** (-9.91)	0.166 *** (25.11)	0.0018 *** (4.91)	-0.050 *** (-6.97)	0.159 *** (6.17)
Fraction employees aged 45-54 in firm's first year	0.00056 *** (7.65)	-0.032 *** (-11.11)	0.085 *** (12.03)	0.0014 *** (3.59)	-0.043 *** (-4.66)	0.101 *** (3.61)
Log(1+firm employees) in firm's first year	0.00039 *** (63.63)	-0.067 *** (-78.92)	-0.222 *** (-125.77)	0.0017 *** (41.69)	-0.035 *** (-14.12)	0.172 *** (-26.06)
Industry fixed effects?	Yes	Yes	Yes	Yes	Yes	Yes
State fixed effects?	Yes	Yes	Yes	Yes	Yes	Yes
Year fixed effects?	Yes	Yes	Yes	Yes	Yes	Yes
N	1,048,366	814,074	301,909	158,643	91,323	35,857
Pseudo-R^2/R^2	0.355	0.032	0.353	0.337	0.052	0.040

Table IX. Within Firm Differences in Wages of Younger and Older Employees

OLS regressions are estimated using the difference log wage (in year 2005 dollars) per employee between two employee age categories as the dependent variable. The independent variables are firm age categorical variables and lagged natural logarithm of 1 plus total firm employees. The firm age category of over 20 years is omitted. Included in each specification are 4-digit SIC code fixed effects, state fixed effects and year fixed effects. The unit of observation is a firm-year. T-statistics adjusted for clustering by firm are reported in parentheses. Panel A reports results for all firms in the union of the LEHD and LBD databases between years 1992 and 2004. Panel B reports results for the sample of public firms. The first two columns report regressions using wages for all employees. The second two columns report regressions using wages for new hires only. ***, **, and * indicate statistical significance at the 1%, 5% and 10% levels, respectively.

Panel A - All Firms

	(1) Difference in log(wage/employee) between 45-54 and 25-34 employee age categories	(2) Difference in log(wage/employee) between ≥ 55 and 25-34 employee age categories	(3) Difference in log(wage/new hire) between 45-54 and 25-34 new hire age categories	(4) Difference in log(wage/new hire) between ≥ 55 and 25-34 new hire age categories
Firm age 1-5 years	-0.157 *** (-93.66)	-0.314 *** (-148.66)	0.006 *** (3.47)	-0.001 (-0.35)
Firm age 6-10 years	-0.097 *** (-62.51)	-0.263 *** (-134.11)	-0.019 *** (-11.82)	-0.017 *** (-7.65)
Firm age 11-15 years	-0.021 *** (-13.38)	-0.182 *** (-90.55)	-0.014 *** (-7.98)	-0.012 *** (-4.97)
Firm age 16-20 years	0.024 *** (16.17)	-0.080 *** (-43.88)	-0.009 *** (-5.19)	-0.007 *** (-2.94)
Lagged log(1+firm employees)	0.013 *** (34.03)	0.016 *** (32.58)	0.007 *** (19.65)	0.005 *** (10.49)
Industry fixed effects?	Yes	Yes	Yes	Yes
State fixed effects?	Yes	Yes	Yes	Yes
Year fixed effects?	Yes	Yes	Yes	Yes
N	6,139,985	5,076,116	2,573,540	1,765,011
R^2	0.026	0.045	0.008	0.029

Panel B - Public Firms

Table X. Supply of Young Workers and the Rate of New Firm Creation

OLS regressions are reported in which the ratio of new firms to all firms in a state or state-industry pair is regressed on the fraction of the state population aged 15 to 24 years, as measured 10 years ago, or the fraction of the state population aged 5 to 15, as measured 20 years ago. The data is from the LBD over the years 1980 to 2000. Coefficients are reported followed by robust t-statistics in parentheses. ***, **, and * indicate statistical significance at the 1%, 5% and 10% levels, respectively.

	(1) New Firm Creation Rate - All Industries	(2) New Firm Creation Rate - All Industries	(3) New Firm Creation Rate - Biotech	(4) New Firm Creation Rate - Biotech	(5) New Firm Creation Rate - Electronics	(6) New Firm Creation Rate - Electronics	(7) New Firm Creation Rate - Telecom	(8) New Firm Creation Rate - Telecom
Fraction of population aged 15 to 25 10 years ago	0.085 ** (1.91)		0.046 ** (1.92)		0.367 *** (4.53)		0.145 (1.55)	
Fraction of population aged 5 to 15 20 years ago		0.120 (1.61)		0.055 * (1.82)		0.264 ** (1.99)		0.096 (1.33)
State fixed effects?	Yes	Yes	Yes	Yes	Yes	Yes	Yes	Yes
Year fixed effects?	Yes	Yes	Yes	Yes	Yes	Yes	Yes	Yes
N	1,020	816	1,020	816	1,020	816	1,020	816
R^2	0.644	0.702	0.555	0.703	0.375	0.609	0.272	0.371

Table A.I. Matching Method for Establishments in the LEHD and the LBD

This table reports the percentage of establishments in the LEHD that are matched to the LBD by the matching method used. Reported in the first column are the percentages of matched establishments in the period 1992 to 2001, for which SIC codes are used to identify an establishment's industry. Reported in the second column are the percentages of matched establishments in the period 2002 to 2004, for which NAICS codes are used to identify an establishment's industry.

	1992-2001		2002-2004
Percentage of establishments matched on EIN, state and county, 4-digit SIC code	66%	Percentage of establishments matched on EIN, state and county, 5-digit NAICS code	58%
Percentage of establishments matched on EIN, state and county, 3-digit SIC code	6%	Percentage of establishments matched on EIN, state and county, 3-digit NAICS code	7%
Percentage of establishments matched on EIN, state and county, 2-digit SIC code	7%	Percentage of establishments matched on EIN, state and county, 2-digit NAICS code	12%
Percentage of establishments matched on EIN, state and county, 1-digit SIC code	8%	Percentage of establishments matched on EIN, state and county, 1-digit NAICS code	6%
Percentage of establishments matched on EIN and state and county	13%	Percentage of establishments matched on EIN and state and county	17%

Table A.II. Match Rates between Establishments in the LEHD and LBD

This table reports the percentage of establishments in the LBD that are matched to the LEHD by year, for those state-years included in the LEHD. Over the period 1992 to 2001, establishments in the LEHD are first matched to the LBD using EIN, state and county, and 4-digit SIC code, then using EIN, state and county, and 3-digit SIC code, then using EIN, state and county, and 2-digit SIC code, then using EIN, state and county, and 1-digit SIC code, and finally using just EIN and state and county. Over the period 2002 to 2004, establishments in the LEHD are first matched to the LBD using EIN, state and county, and 5-digit NAICS code, then using EIN, state and county, 3-digit NAICS code, then using EIN, state and county, and 2-digit NAICS code, then using EIN, state and county, and 1-digit NAICS code, and finally using just EIN and state and county.

	1992	1993	1994	1995	1996	1997	1998	1999	2000	2001	2002	2003	2004	All Years
Match rate between LEHD and LBD	67%	65%	67%	66%	67%	69%	66%	66%	65%	73%	49%	55%	55%	63%

Table A.III. Summary Statistics for Firms Included in the Main Estimation Sample

This table reports means for key variables for the samples of firms used in earlier analysis. Panel A reports means for the sample of 16,343,058 firm-year observations in Table II, Panel A. Panel B reports means for the sample of 11,404,068 firm-year observations in Table IV, Panel A. Employee growth is defined as the annual change in firm-level employees divided by the average employment at the firm over the two years during which the change is measured. For first-year firms, employment in the first year is set equal to zero. For exiting firms, employment in the second year is set equal to zero. Payroll per employee and payroll per new hire are reported in constant year 2005 dollars. Means are reported for all firms in the first column and then by firm age category in subsequent columns as denoted by the column headings.

	All Ages	Ages 1-5	Firm Age Ages 6-10	Ages 11-15	Ages 16-20	Ages >20
	(1)	(2)	(3)	(4)	(5)	(6)
Panel A. All Firms						
Number of employees	26.0	10.2	11.7	16.0	29.2	66.4
Employee growth (including firm deaths)	-0.030	0.230	-0.022	-0.031	-0.021	-0.040
Payroll per employee	27,249	24,903	25,920	27,799	30,115	29,518
Panel B. Hiring Firms						
	(1)	(2)	(3)	(4)	(5)	(6)
Number of employees	38.6	12.5	17.5	24.4	45.2	104.4
Employee growth (including firm deaths)	-0.048	0.201	-0.072	-0.071	-0.050	-0.063
Payroll per new hire	19,986	20,594	18,822	19,395	19,787	20,389

Table A.IV. Summary Statistics for Public Firms Only

This table reports means for key variables for the sample of public firms included in the regressions reported in Table II, Panel B. Means are reported for all firms in the first column and then by firm age category, defined in terms of years from initial public offering (IPO) in subsequent columns as denoted by the column headings. Payroll per employee and payroll per new hire are reported in constant year 2005 dollars. Total assets, sales, and market capitalization are reported in millions of constant year 2005 dollars. Tobin's Q is defined as fiscal year-end market value of equity plus market value of preferred stock plus total liabilities divided by total assets. Leverage is defined as total debt divided by total assets.

Panel A. Public Firms

			Years Since IPO			
	All Years	1-5 Years	6-10 Years	11-15 Years	16-20 Years	>20 Years
	(1)	(2)	(3)	(4)	(5)	(6)
Number of employees in matched LEHD-LBD establishments	2,938.5	461.9	618.6	863.8	2,526.6	5,010.2
Payroll per employee	54,101	69,467	63,488	57,447	53,563	49,445
Payroll per new hire	40,482	48,466	45,643	42,134	38,895	38,124
Total assets	5,671.5	882.0	1,026.9	2,140.6	5,481.7	9,208.8
Sales	2,571.4	410.5	506.9	1,004.6	2,495.3	4,141.5
Market capitalization	3,309.0	905.0	961.5	1,506.8	2,849.1	5,321.1
Tobin's Q	1.67	2.76	2.35	2.03	1.51	1.27
Leverage	0.219	0.173	0.198	0.245	0.221	0.220